GOLDEN GATE SEMINARY LIBRARY

The Evolution of a Revolution

Reflections on Ancient Christianity in its Judaistic, Hellenistic and Romanistic Expressions

JEFFREY L. SEIF, D.Min.
Jewish Studies Chair
Christ For The Nations Institute
Dallas, Texas

UNIVERSITY PRESS OF AMERICA

Lanham • New York • London

Christ For The Nations Institute

Copyright © 1994 by
Jeffrey L. Seif

University Press of America,® Inc.
4720 Boston Way
Lanham, Maryland 20706

3 Henrietta Street
London WC2E 8LU England

All rights reserved
Printed in the United States of America
British Cataloging in Publication Information Available

ISBN 0-8191-9682-7

 The paper used in this publication meets the minimum requirements of American National Standard for Information Sciences—Permanence of Paper for Printed Library Materials, ANSI Z39.48-1984.

To
Zachary Daniel Seif
זכריה בן יוסף הלוי

With a deep sense of affection and admiration I dedicate this book to you. I love you because you are my son—and as such you are very special to me. I admire you because you are a little guy who goes after what he wants and does not stop until he gets it. *Love God and Go for it, Zachary!* The world awaits your contribution.

Table of Contents

Introduction   9

I. The Evolution of a Revolution   21

II. Jewish Apocalyptic Expectation and New Testament Christian Eschatology   57

III. The Roman Christian Re-Interpretation of Sacred Scripture and Sacred Space   131

Conclusion   183

Foreword

Having been born and raised in a Pentecostal-Charismatic home, and having grown up under the shadow of the "anointing," I have come to greatly appreciate the power of a genuine Holy Spirit experience, as well as the value of subjective truth. Both, I believe, give real spiritual vitality to the Christian faith. After growing up and leaving my Pentecostal home, I had the priviledge of attending L'Abri, in Switzerland, and studying under the late Dr. Francis Schaeffer—a Conservative, Christian theologian and philosopher. There, I heard him emphasize over and over again the importance of having a faith that is not purely rooted in subjective truth (feelings, experiences, miracles, etc.). As I think about it all, it seems to me that the Pentecostal movement, with its accent marks on the supernatural, taught me to use my faith—a lesson that I will never forget; Dr. Schaeffer, with his perspective, encouraged me to use my head as well as my faith—a lesson that, likewise, will remain with me throughout my life.

I mention all of this because Dr. Seif, in this his most recent book, begins by, among other things, addressing subjective and objective truth—"Faith and Reason," as he puts it. He, from what I gathered, however, isn't especially concerned with the modern tension—at least not in this book. Here, Jeff is directly concerned with trends and problems in ancient Christianity.

What will you discover in these pages? Jeff's formal research and constructive insights will enable Christians to appreciate their Christian heritage—the Church's "Jewish connection" as Jeff likes to put it. His thorough analysis, likewise, will help Christians better appreciate how Christianity was eventually "disconnected" from Judaism—a fact that Jeff, in various ways and for various reasons, laments.

Frankly, you may not like all of what you read in *The Evolution of a Revolution*—at times, the facts are a bit disturbing; you will, however, appreciate Dr. Seif's having brought the information to your attention. The serious student of church history will find this book to be a valuable addition to their library.

Dennis G. Lindsay
President, CFNI

Introduction

I have been told that when a single grain of sand gets lodged within an oyster it can irritate its adductor muscle and cause the mollusk to produce a pearl—thus, "the *pain* produces the *gain*." I can relate to annoyed oysters—in ways, I was one. Oysters produce pearls to assuage their aggravation; I handle my vexation differently: I write books—and then force my students to buy and read them.

In what follows, in "About the Author," I will begin by sharing some of the *irritations* that irked me and resulted in the production of this book—a *pearl* (Is this a pearl? Maybe, or maybe not—you be the judge). Following immediately, I will explain the volume's title and then I'll go on to explain how the book's story unfolds, and justify why it does so in that particular way—i.e., I will explain *how the oyster will open its mouth to yield its treasure.* Having done the above, I will close by paying tribute to some of the special people who, with me, believed there were some valuable *pearls* contained herein and, accordingly, helped me polish them in the hope that you might come to appreciate their value as well.

A. About the Author
Jewish or Christian?

In the early 70's, during the days of the "Jesus Movement," I met a fellow who convinced me that Jesus Christ was Judaism's promised Messiah. I believed him and became a "Born Again" Christian. In no time, I was informed that I was a *"new creature in Christ"* and that, as such, it was God's will for me to exchange my *old* Jewish family and friends for a *new*

"Christian" network of *spiritual* family members and associates. Accordingly, I opted out of my *old* Jewish world and entered into a *new* Christian one. However, after eight years I was discouraged with my, by then, *not-so-new* Christian world, and felt encouraged to return to the *old* world that I'd abandoned. In short, for a number of reasons, I felt pressed between two worlds—both *old* (Jewish) and *new* (Christian).

Serendipitously, I happened upon a Messianic Jewish community (i.e., a Hebrew Christian congregation) where people attempted to retain the best of both worlds. On the surface, this seemed to be a "Judaism" of sorts: adherents employed *Jewish symbols* and attempted to use *Jewish language* and the like. However, soon I discovered that beneath the *exterior* was an *interior* worldview that seemed *alien* to classical Judaism, and much more akin to Jerry Falwell's "Fundamentalism" and/or "Pentecostalism." I didn't quite know what to make of this possibly oxymoronic Fundamentalist-Christian Jewish religion. Eventually I concluded that Messianic Judaism and I—being a Messianic Jew myself—were in a "twilight zone" of sorts, pressed between two seemingly distinctive and conflicting worlds. My discontent was, in ways, the source of my inspiration. In this regard, Dr. May Sarton, writing in her *Journal of a Solitude,* wrote: "[D]ivine discontent, this disequilibrium, this state of inner tension is the source of artistic energy."[1] I've found this to often be the case with myself.

When I first opened the New Testament I noted how all the actors in the drama were Jews—a fact that *encouraged* me. When I surveyed church history after the New Testament period, I noted how the Jews were, for the most part, all gone—a fact that *discouraged* me. Mindful of this, I've always wondered: What ever happened to the original, Apostolic, New

---

[1] May Sarton, *Journal of a Solitude* (New York: W. W. Norton & Co., 1973), p. 22.

Testament, Jewish Christian church? This book contains some of my work on that question.

In order to attempt to fully answer questions relative to Christian origins one would need to seriously investigate and report of a wide range of contingencies that came into play in the ancient world, and factored into the development of the earliest church(es) within that world (e.g., economic and political forces in the empire; prevalent pagan superstitions, Greek philosophies; Christian heresies, clerical hierarchal developments, councils, creeds, ordinances, controversies, hymns, liturgies). No such full accounting is contained herein. In that I haven't read the primary source material on all of the above, let alone the scholarly discussions containing the various interpretations of those materials, I'm not in a position to present my readers with a comprehensive treatment of the ancient world and church. Nevertheless, I am, I believe, in a position to report on one facet of the ancient Christian milieu: aspects of the rise and demise of ancient Jewish-Christianity.

B. About the Book's Title
The Evolution of a Revolution

Today we live two thousand years removed from the initial events that birthed the Christian religion, and at a time when cultural Christianity—for the most part—occupies center stage in the Western cultural ethos. By way of contradistinction, ancient Christianity was, at first, a misunderstood and despised subculture within the larger Roman culture—hardly the regnant philosophy. Unlike today, in much of the West, Christianity didn't *define* the prevailing norms; rather, it *defied* them! Mindful of this, I prefer to think of ancient Christianity as an *evolving revolutionary movement*, instead of as a formal religious tradition—thus the title "The

Evolution of a Revolution."

Ancient Christianity in its Judaistic, Hellenistic and Romanistic Expressions

"Hebrew (or Aramaic), Greek and Latin" could have worked for my purposes as a subtitle, as could have "Jewish, Greek, or Roman." Of the three, the first—the chosen subtitle—speaks of *cultural distinctives*; the second speaks of *languages*; the third speaks of *national identities*. There are different ways to speak of these three; all are *intrinsically related* and, as you shall see, all are *potentially misleading*.

The late Dr. Erwin Goodenough, professor of religion at Yale University, wrote *Jewish Symbols in the Greco-Roman Period* wherein he demonstrated how ancient Jews "appropriated much of the religiosity of their neighbors."[2] Dr. Martin Hengel, professor of New Testament and early Judaism at the University of Tübingen, recently wrote *The Hellenization of Judea in the First Century After Christ*,[3] wherein he, like Dr. Goodenough, proved that Greek culture had a profound effect on Jewish culture—even more so than had been previously acknowledged. Dr. Joseph Fitzmeyer, an excellent Catholic scholar, in his article "Did Jesus Speak Greek?," makes much of the fact that many Judeans in Jesus' day were trilingual.[4] Writing in *Biblical Archeology Review*, Dr. Pieter W. Van Der Horst informed that 70 percent of the Jewish funerary inscriptions in the Roman world from the Roman period are in Greek, 12 percent are in Latin and only 18 percent in Hebrew.[5] Funeral inscriptions, among other things,

---

[2] Erwin R. Goodenough, *Jewish Symbols in the Greco-Roman Period*, Abridged Edition (Princeton: Princeton University Press, 1988), p. 186.

[3] Martin Hengel, *The Hellenization of Judea in the First Century After Christ* (Philadelphia: Trinity Press International, 1989).

[4] *Biblical Archeology Review* (September/October 1992), pp. 58-63.

[5] *Ibid.*, p. 48.

mark the moment when one passes from this world to the next (to God!). That Jewish testimonies of this crossing appear mostly in Greek and Latin, and rarely in Hebrew or Aramaic, is shocking, and further evidence of the strong hellenistic penetration into the Jewish psyche.

My point here really is quite simple: we are forced to come to terms with the fact that the *boundaries between ancient Jewish and Gentile cultures were blurred.*[6] Given this, I repeat that it is potentially misleading to speak in terms of distinct influences, Jewish, Greek and Roman. If we take this point to be true—and I think we must—then the following question arises with regard to this book: Why bother to speak in terms of any kind of evolution through Jewish, Greek and Roman expressions?

Convinced as I am that Christianity sprang from a Jewish matrix, albeit a Hellenistic-type Judaism, I believe that our journey must begin in Judea—specifically, in understanding the ancient Jewish world. The Gospel message, as we know, spread beyond Israel's borders and on into the Greco-Roman world. Away from Jerusalem, and centered in major cosmopolitan Greek cities, Christianity took on new cultural expressions, owing to the fact that adherents to the Messianic/Christian Faith were predominantly of non-Jewish extract. I am interested in examining aspects of this evolution—in brief. Lastly, when speaking of the Romanistic world, I should say that I have in mind a later era when Christianity was no longer the religion of a despised subculture, but the official religion of the Roman empire's upper classes.

In sum, *the book's title speaks of the ancient Jewish movement's growth and expansion, from its humble beginnings in Judea to its penetration into the world of the pagan elite*

---

[6] See Jacob Neusner's *Judaism in the Matrix of Christianity* (Philadelphia: Fortress Press, 1986); *Judaism in the Beginning of Christianity* (Philadelphia: Fortress Press, 1984).

who governed the Roman empire—as you will see, it was quite a jump and it is quite a story.

C. About the Book
Historical Theology, Jewish Studies & Christian Origins
Historical Theology

Dr. Russell P. Spittler, an Assemblies of God clergyman and a professor at Fuller Theological Seminary, wrote an essay in *The Use of the Bible in Theology: Evangelical Options* wherein he shared how he began his formal training by studying at a Pentecostal Bible college, after which he eventually went on to take a Ph.D. from Harvard University. Significant for him was his discovery of history *after* his initial Bible college days: "[In graduate school—Wheaton] I had discovered historicalness," said Dr. Spittler, "and I would never be the same again."[7] Spittler discovered history and in the process gained access to the Bible's *content* and *context*. I, like Professor Spittler, have discovered history and I, like him, will never be the same. Herein, you are going to discover history too—*Jewish history* as well as *Christian history*—and hopefully you, likewise, will be changed.

Jewish Studies & Christian Origins

Employing Jewish studies to service an inquiry into Christian origins may, for some, sound a bit odd. Here I will ask and answer the following: Can Jewish studies service those engaged in trying to understand early Christian origins?

I am pleased to, among other things, chair a Jewish Studies department at CFNI—a wonderful Charismatic Bible college. At first, as was to be expected, some students wondered whether

---

[7] Russell Spittler, "Scripture and the Theological Enterprise," in *The Use of the Bible in Theology: Evangelical Options*, ed. Robert K. Johnston (Atlanta: John Knox Press, 1985), p. 63.

"Jewish Studies" really belonged in the school's "Christian" curriculum. Some were concerned that the department merely reflected the inclinations of assorted "special interest groups" (e.g., Jewish-Christians, Christians with Zionistic leanings, etc.) and *not* the needs and interests of tomorrow's Christian leaders. In defense, I argued that "Jewish Studies" does perform a service for those engaged in "Christian Studies." In what follows immediately, I will let others argue my case for me.

Dr. Geza Vermes, a distinguished professor at Oxford University, opined: "We will not get the revival of scholarship that we look for until interpreters of the Christian gospels learn to *immerse themselves in the native religion of Jesus the Jew, and in the general climate of the world and age in which he lived.*"[8] Interestingly, Professor Vermes is not alone in his appreciation of the need for Christian theologians to come to terms with Jesus' Jewishness. Another luminary, Professor E. P. Sanders, wrote *Jesus and Judaism,*[9] wherein he concerned himself with ancient Judaism and the early Christian message as well. Dr. James H. Charlesworth, professor of New Testament Language and Literature and Chair of the Department of Biblical Studies at Princeton University, attests to a similar interest in one of his recent books, entitled *Jesus Within Judaism.*[10] I refer to these scholars—and there are *many* others—to evidence that there is indeed an appreciation for Jewish Studies in Christian circles. As you might imagine, I'm pleased by this trend.

Summary

So far, in this subsection, I've extolled the virtues of historical inquiry, and I've posited that Jewish studies renders

---

[8] Italics mine; Vermes, G., *Jesus and the World of Judaism* (Philadelphia: Fortress Press, 1984), p. 73.

[9] Sanders, E. P., *Jesus and Judaism* (Philadelphia: Fortress Press, 1985).

[10] Charlesworth, J., *Jesus Within Judaism* (New York: Doubleday, 1988).

a service to those engaged in studying Christian origins. In what follows immediately, I will argue that eclecticism is another important ingredient in theological inquiry.

Eclecticism & Theological Inquiry

Martin Luther, reflecting on the theological journey, once opined: "The only good theology is the theology of pilgrims. *We are all talking about a person we've never seen and a place we've never been.*" Mindful of his words, I prefer to do my theological work in conversation with *others*—and not just with those who hold to the same presuppositions as I. Simply put, *I try and get what I can from a variety of sources.*

The Roman Catholic church has traditionally placed a special seal—a *Nihil Obstat* and *Imprimatur*—on religious books that it officially deems to be "free of doctrinal or moral error"; thus, books so marked are considered to be spiritually safe for consumption by the masses.[11] So as not to simply single out the Roman Catholic church, I want to note that *all* denominations, likewise, have their own "official" trustworthy sources of information, as well as ways of commending their trustworthiness to their respective constituents. While this is understandable, *I think it is extremely dangerous to require that we only have intellectual relations with members of our own spiritual family*—what I call "intellectual incest." I once heard a preacher say: "I'm Baptist born and Baptist bred, and when I die I'm Baptist dead!" I believe that loyalty is commendable; however, there is absolutely no merit in only allowing oneself to only be informed by official Baptist, Lutheran, Catholic or Pentecostal authorities (to name but a few examples). Organizations that insist that their constitu-

---

[11] I should note that since Vatican II the Roman Catholic church grants that Protestants, and even Jews, can produce books worthy of attention—even though they don't carry the official "seal of approval."

ents only allow themselves to be informed by their own "official sources" usually do so for the purposes of manipualting them—it's as simple as that; such exclusiveness is all too often a subterfuge for vile self-serving institutional interests. *We all need to learn to hear from others.*[12]

Professor Wayne A. Meeks, a church historian at Yale University, wrote that some ancient Christians—like modern ones—had "a shallow self-confidence that purchases its security by excluding inconvenient considerations and inconvenient people." He then advised that we *not* "filter out all but a single way of [hearing and] speaking."[13] My interest in *inclusivity over exclusivity* prompts me to agree with Dr. Meeks. I don't want to write off what someone says simply because they inconveniently challenge notions that I hold to be sacrosanct. I think that I'm all the better for allowing myself to be challenged and stimulated by honest and friendly discussion. For this reason, herein I seek to work in conjunction with *others*—e.g., Catholics, Mainline and Liberal Protestants, non-Charismatic Christians and Jewish theologians—who have similar historical interests but hold to different presuppositions.

In his book *Vision and Discernment*, Dr. Charles Wood, an avowed "Liberal" theologian, correctly noted how all theologians have their own theological dispositions, or prevailing tendencies, which he refers to as their *habitus* (or habit).[14] Here—remembering his point and feeling the need to identify

---

[12] Furthermore, while I'm on the point, let me state emphatically that I have absolutely no tolerance for arrogant self-proclaimed prophets who say that they only allow themselves to, as they put it, "hear from God" and "not man"! *I want to hear from both*—God, of course, being the more important of the two.

[13] Wayne A. Meeks, "The Polyphonic Ethics of St. Paul," *The Annual of the Society of Christian Ethics* (Washington: Georgetown University Press, 1988), p. 24 and p. 27.

[14] Charles Wood, *Vision and Discernment* (Atlanta: Scholars Press, 1985), pp. 26-35.

my own *habitus*—I think it may be helpful for me to spell out the theological world that I personally inhabit. In brief, I understand myself to be a Conservative, Evangelical, Charismatic, Christian theologian of Jewish extract. Being a Conservative, I hold the Bible, and the doctrines contained therein, in the highest regard. Having said that, I wish to again state that, though I am a "Conservative" theologian, myself, herein I have attempted to orchestrate a *polyphonic symphony replete with myriad theological voices.*

Summary

In sum, this book is about Church history. It employs Jewish Studies to service those interested in early Christian history. Lastly, it calls upon the wisdom of a broad range of scholars.

How This Book Unfolds

Here I'd like to discuss how the oyster is going to open its mouth to hopefully give access to its pearl—its treasure. I will do this by first explaining my understanding of what is generally involved in historical writing, after which I'll briefly describe exactly what I am going to do in this volume.

Historiography

Dr. Earle E. Cairns, former distinguished professor of Church history at Wheaton College wrote *God and Man in Time: A Christian Approach to Historiography*, and said:

> The term *historiography* is sometimes used to mean the process of writing history, which includes the [1] gathering of documents; [2.] critical research to validate each document's authenticity, genuineness, and integrity; [3] the interpretation of the data; [4] and the imaginative written restatement of past events. Thus conceived, historiography is the discipline of

historical writing.[15]

Simply put, I have employed Dr. Cairns' four-step program.

The Particulars of this Book
In the first chapter, I am concerned with the rise and demise of the first Jewish-Christian communities. This section, entitled "The Evolution of a Revolution," tells the book's story.

In the following chapter, through an examination of ancient pseudepigraphical literature, I will evidence how Jesus' message on the "Kingdom of Heaven" would likely have been understood by His Jewish contemporaries. Then I'm concerned with the Apostle Paul's innovative translation/ contextualization of that message. As the Gospel advanced beyond Israel's borders, and on into the Greco-Roman world, Paul reasoned that it was necessary to creatively re-work parts of the Messianic-Jewish faith in order to service the needs of his non-Jewish constituents. My interest in Paul's Hellenistic (Greek) world and mission is limited—quite limited: my only intention is to demonstrate that the first Christian message delivered therein was a *radically reformed Jewish message*—something churchmen eventually lost sight of.

In the last chapter, I will consider how that, for the most part, post-Apostolic churchmen—i.e., Church Fathers who followed long after Paul and the Apostolic Era—scorned the original Jewish Christians outright, and made *anti*-Judaism normative in Christian circles. I will examine some of the art, architecture and literature of the regnant imperial Roman Church and note how the Christian faith took on expressions unlike anything the earliest churchmen had ever imagined.

Having done all the above, I trust that I will have exposed my readers to the evolution of the Messianic revolution—i.e.,

---

[15] Earle E. Cairns, *God and Man in Time: A Christian Approach to Historiography* (Grand Rapids: Baker Books, 1977), p. 11.

ancient Christianity in its Judaistic, Hellenistic and Romanistic expressions.

Acknowledgements

Because of the many weaknesses in my thinking and writing, I've asked other professionals to review my manuscript and offer their suggestions for improving it. In addition to the many invaluable services rendered by my wife, Patty L. Seif, B.S., M.Ed., M.A., I'm greatly indebted to the following for their assortrd contributions: Dan Juster, M.Div., Th.D., Richard Hanner Th.B., M.A., David Heath, M.Div., M.A., Al Lostetter, M.D., George Malek, Ph.D., D.Min., Louis Goldberg, M.A., Th.D., Dennis Lindsay, B.S., Marty Waldman, Th. B., Billy Abraham, M.Div., D.Phil., John Garlock, B.S., M.A., to name but a few. I'm especially indebted to Carol Simon, J. D. for her editorial work on an earlier version of the manuscript, and Mr. Paul Butler, a former student of mine and present graduate student in Theology at Perkins Theological Seminary (SMU), for his editorial help with the final draft. Special thanks to Brandon and Becky Blake for technical assitance. Ms. Maurene Lancaster, my liason with the University Press of America, was quite helpful as well.

Last but not least, let me say that *I am also indebted to my many students, past and present, at CFNI.* I've been impressed by the quality of their questions—though, frankly, I haven't always been impressed by the quality of my answers. With their bright and open hearts and minds, they have encouraged me to do my best to serve them. In this volume, I can honestly say that I've given my best. Above all, I hope that my students will be pleased by my work, much as I always hope to be pleased by theirs.

I

The Evolution of a Revolution

Introduction

We will now enter a time-machine and journey back to the dawn of the Christian era. We will chart the original movement's progress (or "regress," as some would say) away from its original "Jewish" form and toward its official Roman "Christian" expression. In what follows we will look at the rise of the Jewish non-Pauline (or pre-Pauline) Messianic movement, as well as the rise of Pauline Christianity which developed as a result of his mission to the Gentiles. Having examined both the rise of the original Jewish-Christian movement, as well as the rise of Paul's outreach to the Greeks, we will then consider the demise of the original Messianic Jewish expression and the triumph and accelerated rise of the Roman Christian Church. If successful, the following reflections should give one an overview of the rise and demise of the original Apostolic church.

A. The Rise of Non-Pauline Messianic Judaism
The Existence of Ancient Non-Pauline Jewish Christianity

In his book *From the Maccabees to the Mishnah*, Jewish history professor Shaye Cohen, of the Jewish Theological Seminary, quotes St. Jerome who said of the early Jewish-Christians: "They are *not* Jews because they believe in Christ, and they are *not* Christians because they observe the Jewish laws."[16] From this we note that Jerome's Messianic Jews sought loyalty in two worlds—Jewish and Christian; for him,

---

[16] Shaye Cohen, *From the Maccabees to the Mishnah* (Philadelphia: Westminster Press, 1989), p. 168.

The Evolution of a Revolution

they had membership in neither. Here I want to ask: *Who were these ancient non-people?* In this section on Messianic Jewish phylogeny, I'll attempt an answer.

I'd like to simply ask and answer the following: Can there be such a thing as *"non-Pauline Christianity"*? The expression "Pauline corpus" is used in theological nomenclature to delineate the body of literature penned by the Apostle Paul. Further subdivided into "doctrinal" and "pastoral" epistles, these "authoritative" documents serve the church, to use the Latin dictum, as part of the *norma normans non normata*[17]— i.e., the standardizing norm for Christian confessional statements and the like.[18] In that Pauline theology has, for centuries, been used to demarcate the boundaries of acceptable Christian orthodoxy and orthopraxis, the notion of a non-Pauline Christian expression, at first, sounds oxymoronic—a contradiction. When considering the possibilities of a "non-Pauline Christianity" *today*, we come to a necessary and immediate dead end street. But what about *yesterday*? Was there ever a non-Pauline Christian expression?

Writing in *Peter, Stephen, James and John: Studies in Early Non-Pauline Christianity*, the late F. F. Bruce, former professor of New Testament at the University of Manchester, took up the question and observed: "It is plain from Paul's own writings that *other* presentations of the Christian message than his own were current during his apostolic career."[19] Professor Bruce is correct. Not only were there "other" bonafide "Christian" expressions, there were "other" expressions that were even hostile to Paul.

In the New Testament we learn that many believers questioned whether Paul had earned the privilege to be an

---

[17] Roger Haight, *Dynamics of Theology* (New York: Paulist Press, 1990), p. 89.

[18] Richard A. Muller, *Dictionary of Latin and Greek Theological Terms* (Grand Rapids: Baker Book House, 1989), p. 203.

[19] Italics mine; F. F. Bruce, *Peter, Stephen, James and John: Studies in Early Non-Pauline Christianity* (Grand Rapids: Eerdmans, 1979), pp. 13-14.

The Evolution of a Revolution

authoritative spokesperson for Messianic faith and praxis. His right to be called an "Apostle" was constantly called into question, owing to the fact that he was *not* an original member of the apostolic community, and thus had no firsthand knowledge of Jesus' life and teachings. Though Paul became the universal church's *main* spokesman, we should recognize that he was *not* the church's *first* spokesman. Worthy of note is the fact that there was a *vibrant*, non-Pauline[20] Messianic Jewish faith *before* Paul ever *believed* in Jesus, *preached* Jesus, and put pen to paper to *write about* Jesus; this other non-Pauline community, of course, had other teachers.[21]

Paul took the Gospel *beyond* Israel's borders, to distant communities, where he successfully "contextualized" it; thus he appropriately became known as the "Apostle to the Gentiles." The honorific title formally gave him the right to speak both *to* and *for* the Gentile churches—*no more*. Unlike today, his authoritative sphere of influence was limited; certainly it *didn't* extend back to Jerusalem, where his seeming antinomianism,[22] reflected by his seemingly perfidious disregard for halachic regulations,[23] greatly disturbed the masses, many of whom were bent on being obedient to the literal teachings promulgated in the Mosaic constitution. While a few of the Judean believers were perhaps appreciative of Paul's innovative cross cultural ministry, it seems that many only tolerated him at best, and that significant segments of the community utterly disdained him.

Owing to the misunderstanding and ensuing controversy, *ancient* Messianic Judaism bifurcated into two primary subdivisions. Dr. Michael Schiffman, of the Union of Messianic

---

[20] *Ibid., passim*.

[21] In fact, we're told that Saul/Paul even persecuted this community.

[22] Paul didn't believe in anarchy. Whether in fact he was an antinomian is open for discussion—frankly, I don't think he was (cf. Rom. 2:13; 7:12); nevertheless, the point here is that the Judean believers thought he was, and this was the source of the tension. For his part, Paul does seem to go out of his way to demonstrate that they were incorrect in their assumption.

[23] Cf., e.g., Galatians, *passim*; Acts 15:1f; 21:15f.

The Evolution of a Revolution

Jewish Congregations, wrote *Return From Exile*, wherein he briefly touched upon the rift.[24] Leaning for the most part on Professor Ray Pritz's work *Nazarene Jewish Christianity* (see below), Dr. Schiffman concluded that the initial group, the "Nazarenes," were made up of moderates who supported Paul; in the other camp, known in antiquity by the appellations "Ebionites" and/or "Elkasites," were fanatics who were unable to resolve their difficulties with the apostle in particular, and Gentile Christianity in general. Dr. Gerd Luedemann, New Testament professor and director of the Institute of Early Christian Studies in the University of Göttingen, penned *Opposition to Paul in Jewish Christianity*, wherein he conjectured that there was a definite *genetic relationship between the various strands of Messianic Judaism, traceable back to the conflict in the first Jerusalem church over the question of Paul's authority and ministry.*[25] All the roads lead back to the Nazarene Messianic Jewish community in Jerusalem, and their problems with Paul and his Gospel.

What was at the heart of the conflict? If "Jewish Christians" are defined as folk who are *primarily concerned with accentuating Jesus' Jewishness,* clearly Paul was *not* one! Modern Messianic believers claim that the Gospel is quintessentially a Jewish story, and therefore fully appropriate for consumption by the Jewish community. By way of contradistinction, we realize that Paul was engaged in demonstrating that this "Jewish" Messiah was really quite appropriate for the "Gentile" community. As such the accent marks were *not* placed on Jesus' Jewishness. Furthermore—and this goes to the heart of the conflict—Paul appeared to them to be advocating a *relaxation* at best, and/or a *cessation* at worst, of the requirements promulgated within the Mosaic Law.

---

[24] Schiffman leans heavily on Ray A. Pritz's work, *Nazarene Jewish Christianity* (Leiden: E. J. Brill, 1988).

[25] Gerd Luedemann, *Opposition to Paul in Jewish Christianity*, trans. M. Eugene Boring (Minneapolis: Fortress, 1989), passim.

The Evolution of a Revolution

This, in the view of many, was tantamount to an abdication of something quite dear to them: their Judaism. The Jerusalem Messianic Jewish community, the Nazarenes, envisioned that Jesus was the *Jewish* Messiah and that, as such, He would both *enhance Israel's prestige* and *fulfill Israel's destiny*—and theirs as well, as children of Israel. To them, Paul understandably seemed to be preaching "another Gospel."

The nature and history of the tensions between Pauline and non-Pauline factions *within* the ancient movement will *not* be pursued here, tempting as that may be. My purpose in raising the matter is to call attention to the following: (1) *there most certainly was a non-Pauline expression of Christianity*; (2) the "other" version of Christianity *pre-dated* the Pauline version; and (3) the "other" version, with whom Paul was at odds, was none other than the *original Jerusalem Church.*

The Rise of Non-Pauline Messianic Judaism

Because we are looking at the original Jewish-Christian movement's rise, I think it would be helpful if we considered their platform. Specifically, we need to know: *what* they believed and *how* they propagated those beliefs.

The *Nazarenes were practicing Jews who believed that Jesus was Israel's promised Messiah.* As we shall see, initially they were perceived as one of several renewal movements *within* Judaism. It was not until later that the situation deteriorated, thus forcing them out of the Jewish fold.

Regarding the propagation of their belief(s), I'd like to begin by postulating the following: the high octane fuel that fired the evangelistic engines of nascent Jewish-Christianity was made up of a blend of *inspired apostolic preaching* mixed with *attendant supernatural giftings.*

Luke penned the New Testament's only historic sequel to the four Gospels and thus became ancient Christianity's official historiographer. In Acts 1:1-8:3, he recorded the

The Evolution of a Revolution

Messianic movement's *inception*; in 8:4-12:25, he informs of the movement's *expansion* throughout Israel and on into Syria; and in 13:1-28:31, Luke adumbrates highlights of *Paul's missionary travels*, giving insights into this wandering evangelist's innovative cross-cultural venture into the Greco-Roman world.

Significant for our purposes is the fact that in Luke's Gospel the word "Spirit" appears 31 times in connection with Jesus' earthly ministry, while in Acts, the word "Spirit" appears 66 times in connection with the birth and spread of nascent Christianity—in *both* Judea and abroad.[26] Luke places a premium on "charismatic" spiritual giftings, and makes much of the fact that the supernatural elements attendant in the Judean proclamation of the Kingdom, under the early leadership of *Peter*, were likewise manifest in *Paul's* ministry. Dr. Stanley Toussaint, professor of Bible exposition at the Dallas Theological Seminary, underscores this very point by noting that in Acts 3:1-11 Peter healed a man lame from birth and in 14:8-18 Paul did likewise; in 5:15-16 Peter's shadow was an agent for healing, and in 19:11-12 handkerchiefs and aprons from Paul likewise evidenced some sort of healing propensity; in 8:9-24 Peter successfully stayed the hand of a sorcerer and in 13:6-11 Paul likewise defeats a satanic minion; lastly, in 9:36-41, Peter was used to raise Dorcas to life and in 20:9-12 Paul duplicated the miracle by raising Eutychus.[27] In Acts, *Luke shows that Paul performed the same miracles as Peter.* Why? Is all this duplication mere coincidence? Frankly, I think not. It is meant to demonstrate God's supernatural hand in Paul's innovative ministry.

That early Messianists placed a premium on "Spiritual power" is evidenced in sources other than the New Testament.

---

[26] The "spirit" likewise appears in deuterocanonical *Jewish* literature—cf., e.g., Jud. 16:14; Wis. 1:7; 7:20; 9:17; 15:11, to name but a few of the many examples; see *A Concordance to the Apocrypha/Deuterocanonical Books of the Revised Standard Version* (Grand Rapids: Eerdman's Publishing, 1983), pp. 396-397.

[27] Stanley Toussaint in *The Bible Knowledge Commentary*, New Testament Edition, ed. John Walvoord and Roy Zuck (Wheaton: Victor Books, 1984), p. 349.

The Evolution of a Revolution

Here now we'll consider one example: the *Odes of Solomon.*

Dr. James H. Charlesworth, professor of New Testament at Princeton Theological Seminary, is an expert in the ancient Judean pseudepigraphal genre. He gathered an impressive collection of erudite palaeographers whose studies now provide us English translations of these ancient Oriental texts, extant in Hebrew, Greek, Latin, Syriac and Coptic forms. Their published work, called *Old Testament Pseudepigrapha,* gives modern students a window into the first century Judean world. Charlesworth translated a hymnbook from the late first century, called *Odes of Solomon*; in his preface he reported that the Odes were "composed somewhere in Palestine and perhaps in Pella, where it seems the earliest Jewish Christians fled before the destruction of Jerusalem [in 70 AD]," and that they were "probably composed around the year 100 AD"[28] He underscores the *Odes'* importance saying: these "provide precious reminders of the *first attempts to articulate the unparalleled experience of the advent of the Messiah.*"[29] Let's now consider these *ancient* Messianic Jewish articulations.

In Ode 6:1-2 the psalmist says: "As the [wind] moves through the harp and the strings speak, So the Spirit of the Lord speaks through my members...." In 15-16, he goes on to say that those who are the vehicles for God's Spirit perform miracles: "Blessed are the ministers of that [spiritual] drink... Lives who were about to expire, they have seized from death. And members which had fallen, they have restored and set up." In Ode 18:1 the Messianic psalmist is very explicit: "*Infirmities fled from my body,* and it stood firm for the Lord by His will; because his kingdom is sure." Lastly, the belief in healing is further corroberated in Ode 25:8-9, where the psalmist says: "I was covered with the covering of your spirit, and I removed from me my garments of skin. Because your right

---

[28] "Odes of Solomon" in *Old Testament Pseudepigrapha,* Vol. II., ed. James H. Charlesworth (Garden City: Doubleday & Company, 1985), p. 727.

[29] Italics mine; *Ibid.*

The Evolution of a Revolution

hand raised me, and *caused sickness to pass from me.*"[30]

The psalmist was thankful for God's *"right hand"* raising him from sickness and death. In response, the hymn writer later sings, in Ode 21:1: *"I raised my arms on high* on account of the grace of the Lord." Ode 27:1-2 is even more explicit in this regard: *"I extended my hands and hallowed my Lord;* for the expansion of my hands is his sign" (cf. 42:1-2).[31] The same is repeated again in Ode 37:1: *"I extended my hands toward the Lord,* and toward the Most High I raised my voice."

The textual evidence does seem to suggest that *ancient Messianic Jews were involved in an experience akin to the present Charismatic scene*—though by no means necessarily identical. They placed a premium on "spiritual gifts" and believed that *healing power was an authenticating criterion for leaders* within their communities. This was apparently so much the case that legalisitic pneumatics within the Judean community attacked Paul on the grounds that he *didn't* manifest enough "Spiritual power." The Pauline epistles come replete with ubiquitous examples of Paul's having to ward off threats posed by other traveling evangelists[32] from Judea, who his constituents in the diaspora.[33]

---

[30] Further evidence of "healings" can be culled from a surprising source: the *Mishna*. The fourth volume of the *Mishna* contains a tractate called *Sanhedrin*. Note the following article of excommunication: And these are they that [will] have no share in the world to come... one who reads the *heretical books*, or he that *utters a charm over a wound and says, I will put none of the diseases upon thee, which I have put upon the Egyptians: for I am the Eternal that healeth thee.* [Culled from Philip Blackman's *Mishnayoth*, Vol. IV [Gateshead: Judaica Press, 1983], p. 285.) That this invective was aimed at Messianic Jews is obvious. One need only ask: Who might have had books deemed heretical? and Who might have prayed over wounds claiming promises like "I am the Lord that healeth thee!"? Presumably, the writer had a Messianic Jewish community in view. In that the New Testament canon had not yet been formalized, the "heretical books" needn't necessarily refer to that particular collection of documents; it could also be a reference to other liturgical texts like the Odes of Solomon, above.

[31] Worthy of note is the fact that the "sign" refers to the Cross. A good treatment of this is found in Richard Milborn's chapter "Signs and Symbols," in his *Early Christian Art and Architecture* (Berkley and Los Angeles: University of California Press, 1988), pp. 1-7.

[32] Gerd Theissen treats the subject of traveling evangelists in his *Sociology of Early Palestinian Christianity* (Philadelphia: Fortress, 1985), pp. 8-16; see below.

The Evolution of a Revolution

In Paul's second epistle to the Corinthihian church, we find him embroiled in a dispute over his authority. According to Paul, the Corinthian community was beguiled by an incursion of anti-Paulinists who sought to undermine his apostleship.[34] That Paul was placed on the defensive by charges of a lack of "spiritual giftings," is clearly evidenced. In 2 Cor. 12:1, Paul says "I [too] will go on [to speak of] *visions* and *revelations of the Lord*"; in v. 11b he retorts: "I am not in the least inferior to those superlative apostles"; and in v. 12 Paul explains why he isn't inferior: "The *signs* of a true apostle were *performed* among you... with *signs* and *wonders* and *mighty works*." That Paul was up against folk claiming that he was spiritually impotent—i.e., *non*-Charismatic—is further attested in 13:3, where he says: "since you desire *proof* that Christ is speaking in me." The evidence suggest that Paul was forced on the defensive by traveling preachers who troubled the community by insisting that Paul didn't have what it takes to be a *real* Apostle—i.e., supernatural gifts. Paul responded by reasserting that he does in fact possess the miraculous giftings that both attend and authenticate the Messianic message.

Here again, we are confronted with early Christian polemics; and here again, I must say that I'm *not* especially interested in explicating the various aspects of the diatribe. Worthy of note, for our purposes here, is the fact that the

---

[33] Dr. Abraham Malherbe, professor of New Testament criticism and interpretation at the Yale University Divinity School and author of *Social Aspects of Early Christianity,* wrote: "Contemporary New Testament scholarship has recognized the importance of *wandering preachers* who *challenged* Paul's congregations after he had left them." (Abraham Malherbe, *Social Aspects of Early Christianity* [Philadelphia: Fortress, 1983], p. 65.) Professor Malherbe went on to inform: *"Travel caused confrontations between Christians of different viewpoints,* and we are the richer for them because they make us aware of the diversity that characterized early Christianity." Dr. Gerd Theissen, in his *Sociology of Early Palestinian Christianity,* explicated the significant role played by travelling "prophets" and "teachers," and refuted the notion that "wandering charismatics," as he called them, were only a "marginal phenomenon"; to the contrary, according to him they were the church's "decisive authorities," even in the sub-apostolic era. (Gerd Theissen, *Sociology of Early Palestinian Christianity,* pp. 9-10)

[34] Gerd Luedemann, *Opposition to Paul in Jewish Christianity,* p. 94.

The Evolution of a Revolution

"supernatural" ingredient played a significant role in the rise of early Christianity—both in Judea and in the disapora.

In sum, I have here tried to show that the "Gospel of the Kingdom" is quintessentially a *Jewish* message,[35] and that that Kingdom's arrival was both *preached by Jews* and *authenticated by assorted miracles performed by Jews.*

B. The Demise of Non-Pauline Messianic Judaism

In what follows we will consider some of the major *internal* and *external* forces that, to quote Dr. Michael Schiffman, sent Messianic Judaism "into exile." Here we will call upon a wide range of specialists—e.g., archeologists, patristic historiographers, and the like—who, in their own unique ways, can inform us about Messianic Judaism's mysterious *rise* and *demise*. In what follows, I'll begin with a brief discussion on the precariousness of first century Judean life, after which I'll then rapidly move to the fourth century, where I'll then close with a brief consideration of the tensions between Gentile and Jewish forms of Christianity.

The Precariousness of Life in First Century Judea

Messianic Judaism came into its own in a first century Judean society wracked by *political intrigue, social unrest* and *misguided religious fervor.* Jesus entered this boiling caldron and preached a message of peace and reconciliation. His followers likewise were a moderate voice in this tempestuous climate.[36] Jewish believers were known for their frequenting the Temple and their moderate stance on the taxation issue, in that they advocated the paying of taxes to both God (i.e., Temple) and Caesar (i.e., Rome). For these and other reasons,

---

[35] Dr. Brad Young's *The Jewish Background to the Lord's Prayer* (Austin: Center For Judaic-Christian Studies, 1984) is quite helpful here. See chapter II. C.

[36] Writing in *Sociology of Early Palestinian Christianity*, Dr. Gerd Theissen asserts that "In unruly [first century] Palestine the Jesus Movement was actually one of the conciliatory, moderate groups." (*The Sociology of Early Palestinian Christianity* trans. John Bowden [Philadelphia: Fortress Press, 1978], p. 60.)

The Evolution of a Revolution

ancient *Messianic Judaism shouldn't be considered as merely a quasi-Jewish fringe group operating at the periphery of ancient Judean society.*[37] Like most Judeans of the day, they too were frustrated by Jewish aristocratic perfidy and Roman insensitivity; but, for the most part, they envisioned that the day's problems would be solved when the "Kingdom of God" would be *fully* manifest: their answer was *religious* and not *political*. Believing the "Prince of Peace" would return and inaugurate the Messianic era, they chose to *not* join the ranks of the resistance movement, led by fanatical nationalists seeking political answers to the day's pressing problems.

For years, resistance fighters called "Zealots" had been traversing the countryside pressing the weary populace to resist the religious and secular aristocracies holding sway over the Jewish nation. Vociferously, they urged folk to throw off the imperial Roman yoke, brought to bear through excessive taxation and political mismanagement.[38] When war finally broke out, hordes of these misguided, frenzied nationalists entered Jerusalem, usurped authority and terrorized the general populace. Josephus informs that these "Zealots" called themselves "*Benefactors* and *saviours* of the city."[39] However, when all was said and done, these "benefactors" failed to save the people and the city, and they failed to save their own wretched lives: thanks to them, *Jerusalem was destroyed.*

Jewish Believers in Jesus in First Century Judea

Wisely, the Messianic Jews didn't take part in the suicidal struggle; they temporarily left Jerusalem as Vespasian's Roman armies advanced on the city. Their departure is attested by

---

[37] See Gerd Theissen, *The Sociology of Early Palestinian Christianity* trans. John Bowden (Philadelphia: Fortress Press, 1978), p. 55.

[38] Theissen correctly believes that "Refusal to pay taxes was the decisive cause of the Jewish rebellion." *The Sociology of Early Palestinian Christianity*, p. 43; he bases the belief on Josephus; *De Bello Judaico* BJ 5.9.4. §405; 2.17.1, §405.

[39] *De Bello Judaico* 4.3.5. §146; cited in Theissen's *The Sociology of Early Palestinian Christianity*, p. 51.

The Evolution of a Revolution

Eusebius[40] as well as by Epiphanius.

Eusebius informs:

> The people of the church in Jerusalem were commanded by an oracle given by revelation before the war, to those in the city who were worthy of it, to *depart and dwell in one of the cities of Perea which they called Pella.* (Hist. Ecc. 3.5.3.)

Epiphanius—an anti-Judaic bishop of Jewish extract—likewise attests to their flight, saying:

> When the city was about to be taken by the Romans it was revealed in advance to all the disciples by an angel of God that they should *remove from the city,* as it was going to be completely destroyed. They *sojourned as emigrants to Pella...* in Transjordania... (But after the destruction of Jerusalem, when they returned... *they wrought great signs.* (Treatise on Weights and Measurements* 15)

Here again we're told that these believers wrought "signs." At this juncture, however, I don't want to accentuate their "charismatic" orientation—I've already done that; rather, I simply want to note how *after* the catastrophe in 70 A.D., *the Messianic Jewish survivors returned to Jerusalem to rebuild both their synagogue and their lives.* In this regard, Eusebius informs that they remained in Jerusalem for sixty years:

> [D]own to the invasion of the Jews under Adrian [Hadrian], there were fifteen successions of bishops in that church, all of which they say were Hebrews... at that time the whole church under them consisted of

---

[40] Here I'm relying on Gerd Luedmann's translation in his "Literary Analysis of the Explicit Pella Texts," in his *Opposition to Paul in Jewish Christianity,* trans. by Vandenhoeck & Ruprecht (Minneapolis: Fortress, 1989), p. 203.

The Evolution of a Revolution

faithful Hebrews who continued from the time of the apostles until the seige that then took place.

In sum, it is to be observed that the Judean Messianic believers found themselves pressed amidst the turbulence of their trying times. They were "moderates" who were unable to join ranks with the "resistance movements." Accordingly, they *departed* Jerusalem in advance of the scourge and then *returned* after the war, *rebuilt their synagogue,* and continued preaching and manifesting the Gospel of the Kingdom of God.

Headquarters of the First Century Messianic Community

Some modern archeologists claim to have located the actual headquarters of the ancient Messianic Jewish movement in Jerusalem. The following, most of which is reconstructed from a feature article in *Biblical Archeology Review,* should be of interest in this regard.

In 1948, during Israel's "Independence War," Mount Zion and its environs was a staging area for a considerable amount of fighting between Israeli and Jordanian forces. In the course of the escalating hostilities a mortar shell inadvertantly fell on the traditional Jewish site of King David's tomb. The explosion caused some damage and exposed a section of the building previously hidden from view. In 1951 an Israeli archeologist, Jacob Pinkerfield, was entrusted with the task of surveying the site and repairing the damage. His examination of the site, as you'll see, was quite revealing.

Underneath the existing flooring Pinkerfield found a twelfth century Crusader pavement, beneath which lay a mosaic floor from the fifth century Byzantine period. Just four inches below the Byzantine mosaic, he uncovered the remains of a synagogue's flooring, dating to the first century AD.[41]

---

[41] The evidence seems to suggest that this synagogue was leveled by the Romans and then rebuilt following the Jewish revolt against Rome, in 66-70 C.E.. Coins dating from 67 and 68 A.D. were found on the steps of the building's mikveh, indicating that the synagogue was in use during the first Jewish revolt

The Evolution of a Revolution

Additionally, on the same stratum as the first century synagogue, Pinkerfield unearthed fascinating inscriptions on plaster, and promptly turned them over to the authorities for examination. Oddly, the inscriptions were kept from public view; and after Pinkerfield's death they almost faded into obscurity—this time beneath the rubble of political intrigue.

Happily, the inscriptions were eventually made public, owing to the influence and expertise of Franciscan monks at the Studium Biblicum Franciscanum: professors Testa and Bagatti. Perhaps the delay in publishing the finds can be attributed to their controversial nature: One of the graffiti has the Greek initials for "conquer, savior, mercy"; and the other reads: "O Jesus, that I may live; O Lord of [David] the Autocrat." For this and other reasons, the Fransicans conjecture that buried beneath the present alleged "Tomb of King David" are the ruins of a first century *Messianic Jewish synagogue*.[42]

There are ubiquitous testimonies from antiquity confirming the Fransicans' claim that the disciples returned after the war and built a Messianic synagogue, and that—as fantastic as it sounds—it's this synagogue that is buried beneath what's today called "King David's Tomb." To this very day, Jews visit the first floor of the structure and pray over David's tomb, while Christian pilgrims frequent the second floor and venerate the site believed to be the first actual Messianic Jewish gathering place—known to Roman Catholics as the

---

against Rome. That these coins were found beneath layers of debris, evidences that the building must have fallen during the Jewish war.

[42] Bargil Bixner, "Church of the Apostles Found on Mount Zion," *Biblical Archeological Review* (May/June, 1990), p. 24; see n. 22 on p. 60 for his source: Bellarmino Batti, *The Church From the Circumcision* (Jerusalem: Franciscan Printing Press, 1971), p. 121. Additionally, Professor Pinkerfield concluded that the find was a Jewish synagogue because the structure's niche—where the Torah may have been kept—was oriented toward the Temple Mount, (Bixner, "Church of the Apostles Found on Mount Zion," p. 24) as was normal for synagogues. However, the niche *doesn't* precisely point to the Temple Mount; though it does point in that general direction, it's oriented more precisely toward the present site of the Church of the Holy Sepulchre, believed then to be the site of the crucifixion, burial and resurrection of Christ. Bixner believes that these Messianic Jews oriented their synagogue toward Golgotha.

The Evolution of a Revolution

"Church of the Apostles."

Their case is, in part, built on the following testimony of Bishop Epiphanius, the fourth century bishop mentioned earlier in conjunction with the Nazarenes and the Messianic Jewish flight to Pella. Epiphanius knew that the Messianic Jews *returned* and *rebuilt* their synagogue on Mount Zion.

> [When the emperor Hadrian visited Jerusalem in 130/131 A.D., there was standing on Mount Zion] *a small church of God. It marked the site of the "Upper Room" to which the disciples returned from the Mount of Olives...* (*Treatise on Weights and Measures* 14).

Because the program of building Roman Christian churches in Jerusalem *wasn't* begun until Constantine's era (the fourth century), that "small church of God" mentioned was likely a synagogue of Messianic Jewish origin.

This belief is corroborated by Euthychius, the tenth century Patriarch of Alexandria, who informed that the Jewish believers "returned to Jerusalem in the fourth year of the emperor Vespasian, *and built there their church.*"[43] Eusebius—whom we heard from previously—wrote, in *Demonstratio Evangelica*, of the Gospel that is "poured forth from Jerusalem and Mount Sion adjacent to it,"[44] thus evidencing that he was aware of the Messianic structure on Zion. The facility was also mentioned by Eucherius, a converted Roman senator who became the archbishop of Lyons. Based on St. Jerome's testimony, Eucherius writes: "The plain upper part [of Mount Zion] is occupied by monks' cells which surround a church. Its foundations, it is said, have been laid by the

---

[43] Italics mine. Bargil Bixner, "Church of the Apostles Found on Mount Zion," *Biblical Archeological Review*, p. 26; from Migne, ed., *Patrologia* Vol. III (Paris, 1844), p. 985.

[44] Bargil Bixner, "Church of the Apostles Found on Mount Zion," p. 29; from Baldi, *Enchiridion Locorum Sanctorum* (Jerusalem: Franciscan Printing Press, 1982); reprint of the second edition of 1955), 728.

The Evolution of a Revolution

Apostles... It was there that they were filled with the Spirit of the Paraclete as promised by the Lord."[45] Additionally, Cyril, bishop of Jerusalem, in 384 A.D., delivered a famous sermon in the newly constructed Church of the Holy Sepulchure, and said: "[I]t would have been *more* appropriate to speak about the Holy Spirit in the very place where the Holy Spirit descended upon the Apostles, namely "in the Upper Church of the Apostles."[46] Apparently there were two churches of renown in Jerusalem. Cyril knows that the Holy Spirit originally descended on the one other than the Church of the Holy Sepulchure, that is, at the Church of the Apostles.

Tensions Between the Gentile Christians and the Original Jewish "Christians"

Why didn't Cyril then preach in the church of the original Apostles if he knew of it? Franciscan scholar Dr. Bargil Bixner informs that "Epiphanius also declared that [the church at] *Mt. Zion, which was once a privileged height, had now been 'cut off' (as heretical) from the rest of the church.*"[47] Bixner opines that there had been a *sharp division* between the two communities: the Messianic Jews at the Church of the Apostles and the Greco-Roman Christians at the Church of the Holy Sepulchure, and that the Messianic Jews were *excommunicated* by the Roman church. The bitter tensions mentioned earlier, between the Jewish and Gentile arms of nascent Christianity, came full term in the fourth century—as we shall see.[48]

---

[45] Italics mine; Bargil Bixner, "Church of the Apostles Found on Mount Zion," p. 28; from Baldi, *Enchiridion*, no. 735.

[46] Bargil Bixner, "Church of the Apostles Found on Mount Zion," p. 28.

[47] *Ibid.*, pp. 29-31.

[48] Dr. Robert Milburn, professor of church history at Oxford University, wrote *Early Christian Art and Architecture*, and informed that the ancient *Roman* Christians were *enthralled by the Roman triumph*, and that their cathedral, the Church of the Holy Sepulchure, was a monument to that *victory*. In fact, Professor Milburn says that "they likened it [i.e., the Church of the Holy Sepulchure] to the *New Jerusalem*, foretold by the Prophets and appearing in the visions of the Apocalypse where the throne of God and of the Lamb is seen to *supplant the Temple of the Ancient Law*." (Robert Milburn, *Early Christian Art &*

The Evolution of a Revolution

Leaning on his patristic sources, Bixner informs that the two communities were eventually reconciled owing to the mediation of a Christian of Jewish extract, known as Saint Porphyrius, the bishop of Gaza. The reconciliation resulted in the assimilation of the *moderate* Messianic Jews *within* the Catholic church at large, and was finalized when John II, the bishop of Jerusalem from 387-419 A.D., formally blessed the altar of the Messianic Jews—referred to by him as a *kapporet!* In honor of the unification, Bishop John II gave an astonishing sermon full of Judeo-Christian symbolism, praising Porphyrius for beginning the work of reconciling the two communities.[49]

It's sad that *this "reconciliation" really meant very little.* With Roman Christianity's rise to prominence in the empire, another threat loomed on the horizon: this one would prove more devastating to the Judean Messianic believers than all the previous Roman wars combined. The conciliatory gesturing in Jerusalem was all well and good; but in another city the Roman church was planning a final assault on the Jews: *they schemed to crush all the Jews that they couldn't absorb!* In what follows, I will touch upon anti-Judaism in the Roman state, anti-Judaism in the Roman church, and then anti-Messianic Judaism in the early Roman Catholic church.

Anti-Judaism in the Roman State and Church
Anti-Judaism in the Roman State

The Jews had problems in the Roman world *before, during,* and immediately *after* the New Testament period. Valerius Maximus informed that all Jews were expelled from Rome by Cornelius Hispanus, along with all Chaldaic and Asiatic astrologers from the Orient. However, within 100 years, during the time of Cicero, many Jews made their way back to Rome.

Architecture [Berkley and Los Angeles: University of California Press, 1988], p. 102) Their point was obvious: *the Messianic Jews had to be eliminated if they were going to prevail.*

[49] *Ibid.*, p. 31; from Van Esbroeck's "Jean II de Jerusalem," *Antalecta Bollaniana* 102 (1984), pp. 99-133.

The Evolution of a Revolution

Although tolerated by Augustus, their religion appeared to the Romans as a "barbaric superstitution" and they were the object of much scorn and derision. Under Tiberius, Caligula and initially Claudius, Jews were able to make some advances; however, as has often been the case, official toleration ended with Caesar Claudius' edict in 49 calling for another massive expulsion of Jews from Rome. By the time Nero came to power in 54, the anti-Jewish measures were taken back, owing perhaps to Seneca's positive influence that prevailed in his administration—at first.[50]

Anti-Judaism in the Roman Church

For the most part, the Romans had been tolerant of the Jews; however, the situation began to change when the empire's emperor "saw the light," embraced a form of Christianity himself, and eventually made it the official religion of the empire. That the emperor became a "Christian" was an unprecedented event; understandably, many marvelled and asked: What might God be up to in all of this? Some Christians reasoned that the Kingdom of God would now become manifest on the earth, and that finally "the earth would be full of the knowledge of the Lord as the waters cover the sea." Yale University's late professor Dr. Erwin R. Goodenough opined that the euphoria served to intoxicate many churchmen, some of whom, says Goodenough, began to dream of the church as "being the ideal *rulership* for the world."[51]

Eusebius notes that the "Christian" conquest—both spiritual and material—of the Roman state was understood to be a fulfillment of prophetic "ancient [scriptural] declar-

---

[50] Dr. Wolfgang Wiefel's "The Jewish Community in Ancient Rome and the Origins of Roman Christianity," in *The Romans Debate*, ed. Karl Donfried (Peabody, Mass: Hendrickson Publishers, 1991), pp. 85-101.

[51] *The Church in the Roman Empire* (New York: Henry Holt, 1932; reproduced in New York by Cooper Square Publishers); from Jacob Neusner, *Judaism and Christianity in the Age of Constantine*, p. 16.

The Evolution of a Revolution

ations." In this regard, he says, not

> by hearsay merely or report, but [we] observe... in very deed and with our own eyes that *the declarations recorded long ago are faithful and true...* 'as we have heard, so we have seen, in the city of the Lord of hosts, in the city of our God.' And in what city but in the newly built and god-constructed one, which is a 'church of the living God.'[52]

The following, also from the mind and pen of Eusebius, should prove quite revealing as well. Eusebius was a panygerist; as such, he was invited to give a tricennial oration in honor of the Emperor Constantine. The following is an extract from his speech:

> [B]y the appointment of the Caesars, He [God] *fulfills the predictions of the divine prophets,* which ages and ages ago proclaimed that "the saints of the Most High shall take up the Kingdom.[53]

In short, Eusebius envisioned that Constantine's "conversion" and official endorsement of the Christian religion would serve as the catalyst for the full manifestation of God's Kingdom on Earth. He envisioned that all the prophetic utterances in the First Testament—related to Israel's future, etc.—were to be *fulfilled in and through the Roman Church.*[54] Epiphanius likewise shared this optimistic view—as did most others.

---

[52] Italics mine; *Church History,* trans. Arthur Cushman McGiffert, in *Select Library of the Nicene and Post-Nicene Fathers of the Christian Church,* ed. Philip Schaaf and Henry Wace (Grand Rapids: Eerdmans), p. 369; gleaned from Jacob Neusner, *Judaism and Christianity in the Age of Constantine,* p. 30

[53] Italics mine; H. A. Drake, *In Praise of Constantine* (Berkeley: University of California Press), p. 87.

[54] This is what is referred to today as "Replacement Theology"—i.e., an ideology that sees the church as having usurped literal Israel and, in the process, declaring the Jews as forever vanquished from God's economy.

The Evolution of a Revolution

Constantine's conversion was quite dramatic, and was accompanied by a number of "official" heated invectives against the Jews. Nevertheless, *his policies were not nearly as devastating as his diatribe.* After Constantine's death, his son Constantius II (337-61) pursued anti-Jewish policies with much more vigor, prompting the Jews to oppose his viceroy Gallus in 351-353. His successor, emperor Julian (called the "Apostate") had an altogether different agenda: he endeavored to displace the church and chart a course back to the pre-Christian, pagan days. For this reason and owing to his ambition to exploit Persia—and needing for the latter to protect his rear (in Israel) as he advanced eastward—Julian enlisted the support of the Jews. Julian even allowed them to rebuild the Temple—a project that came to nought owing to the fact that work on the substructure released inflammable gases.[55] *Following Julian's death, anti-Judaic fervor again surfaced*—all the more now, owing to the fact that the church feared the threat of a similiar attempt to *check its gains* and *reduce its claims.*

The deterioration of relations between church and synagogue was kept in check under the emperors Theodosius I[56] (379-395) and Eutropius (395-399); but, as Dr. Michael Grant notes in his *Jews in the Roman World*, the attitudes of St. Ambrose (d. 397), St. John Chrysostom (d. 407), St. Augustine (d. 430) (see chapter VI.) and St. Cyril of Alexandria (d. 444) were *sharply anti-Jewish*. Professor Grant went on to suggest that it was Theodosius II, in 438, who systematized numerous

---

[55] For evidence of the power of explosive gas, one need only reflect on the recent explosion in Guadalajara, Mexico. The disaster took place on 4/22/92. The death toll was near 200; 1,450 were injured; over 1,000 homes and businesses were destroyed.

[56] The rising tide of Christian anti-Semitic fervor is manifested in the following correspondence of Theodosius I, who seeks to defend the Jews against "overzealous" Christians, in 398: "...Your sublime excellency will, therefore, upon receipt of this order, check with appropriate severity the overzealousness of those who, in the name of the Christian faith, arrogate to themselves illegal [powers] and attempt to destroy and despoil synagogues." (see Salo Wittmayer Baron, *A Social and Religious History of the Jews,* Vol. 2 of *Ancient Times* [Philadelphia: Jewish Publication Society, 1952], p. 192; from Jacob Neusner, *Judaism and Christianity in the Age of Constantine,*p. 20).

The Evolution of a Revolution

restrictions against the Jews, and that from then on the situation kept going from bad to worse.[57]

Anti Messianic-Judaism in the Roman Church
Epiphanius

Epiphanius (c. 315-403) was born in Eleutheropolis (*Beit Guvrin*) in Judea. His native tongue was Syrian, but he also knew Greek and Latin as well as Coptic and Hebrew. He studied in Egypt after which he returned to Judea and set up a monastery. He taught there for 30 years until he was elected Bishop of Constantia (Salamis) in 367. He was especially known for his work entitled *panarion,* or *Refutation of All Heresies*. From Epiphanius' vantage point, as we shall see, Nazarenes—the original Jewish believers—were *heretics.*

Following are quotes extracted from Epiphanius' *Against All Heresies* (29) in which he assails the ancient Jewish believers in Jesus—whom he appropriately calls "Nazarenes."[58] In what follows, the italics indicate statements that I wish to accentuate and that I'll pick up on in my commentary that will follow.

Regarding the name of the earliest Jewish Christians, Epiphanius says the following:

> [1,2] They did not give themselves the name of Christ, or that of Jesus, but they called themselves Nazarenes. [1,3] *All Christians were called Nazarenes once.* [5,4]

---

[57] In 395 Theodosius declared that in effect the empire was to be a Christian state; he sought to remove pagan influences and oppose Jews (see Jacob Neusner, *Judaism and Christianity in the Age of Constantine,*p. 23). Sadly, anti-Judaism became a permanent fixture in both church and state. Grant observed: "...official hostility against the Jews, remained inexorable. When the bones of Jewish dead were burnt in a conflagration of the Antioch synagogue, the emperor Zeno (474-491) remarked: 'Why did they not burn the living Jews along with the dead?'" (Michael Grant, *The Jews in the Roman World,* p. 287).

[58] The *Panarion* was extracted from Ray Pritz, *Nazarene Jewish Christianity: From the End of the New Testament Period Until Its Disappearance in the Fourth Century* (Jerusalem: The Magnes Press of the Hebrew University, 1992), pp. 30-35, with the biographical data from p. 29.

The Evolution of a Revolution

> They [i.e., the Iessaioi (see below)] were so-called followers of the apostles, but I suppose that they were Nazarenes, who are described by me here. *By birth they are Jews* and *they dedicate themselves to circumcision.* [5,6] ...after having *heard the name of Jesus only, and having seen the divine signs performed by the hands of the apostles* [—earlier, in 4,9 he said that the name Jesus means "healer" and "physician"—] *they also believed in Jesus.*

With regard to their customs he informs:

> [6,1] [E]veryone called the [first] Christians Nazarenes, as I said before. [7,1] [The problem with these people, was that, in truth] *they remained wholly Jewish and nothing else.* [7,2] *For they use not only the New Testament but also the Old*, like the Jews... They are not at all mindful of other things but *[they] live according to the preaching of the Law as among Jews...* [7,3] *They also accept the resurrection of the dead* and that everything has its origin in God. *They proclaim one God and his Son Jesus Christ.* [7,4] They have a good mastery of the Hebrew language. [7,5] Only in this respect do they differ from Jews and Christians: *with the Jews they do not agree because of their belief in Christ,* [and] *with the Christians because they are trained in the Law of circumcision, the Sabbath and other things.*

As far as their location goes, he notes:

> [7,7] This *heresy of the Nazarenes* exists in Beroea in the neighborhood of Coele Syria and the Decapolis in the region of Pella and in the Basanitis in the so-called Kokabe, Chochabe in Hebrew. [7,8] For *from there it took its beginning after the exodus from Jerusalem when all the disciples went to live in Pella because Christ had told them to leave Jerusalem and to go away since it would undergo a seige. Because of this advice they lived in Perea after having moved to that*

The Evolution of a Revolution

place, as I said. There the Nazarene heresy had its beginning.

With regard to the nature of their crime—i.e., that they were still Jews—we are told:

> [8,1] But *these also have erred in boasting of circumcision,* and such are still "under a curse" not being able to fulfill the Law. [8,5] For thus it is with every heresy, often *trying to outdo each other in the matter prescribed concerning the keeping of the Sabbath and circumcision and other things, even though our Lord freely gave us a more perfect way.*

Speaking of their relationship with other Jews, Epiphanius tells of their rejection:

> [9,1] The brevity of this exposition will also be sufficient for this heresy. For such people make a fine object to be refuted and are easy to catch, for they are rather Jews and nothing else. [9,2] However, *they are very much hated by the Jews.* For not only the Jewish children cherish hate against them but the people also stand up in the morning, at noon, and in the evening, three times a day and they pronounce curses and maledictions over them when they say their prayers in the synagogues. *Three times a day they say: "May God curse the Nazarenes."* [9,3] For *they are more hostile against them because they proclaim as Jews that Jesus is the Christ, which runs counter to those who still are Jews who do not accept Jesus.* [9,4] *They have the entire Gospel of Matthew in Hebrew.* It is carefully preserved by them in Hebrew letters, as I wrote in the beginning... [9,5] Now that we have exposed this heresy as weak and the cause of pain by wasp's poison, and having crushed it with the truth, let us go on to what remains, Beloved, asking God for help.

The Evolution of a Revolution

Epiphanius notes that the earliest Christians—better "Jewish believers"—were called "Nazarenes": "All Christians were called Nazarenes once" (1,3). The appellation "Christian" evolved out of Χριστιανόςοί and was first used by "outsiders" to refer to "insiders" within the messianic movement in Antioch. The name "Nazarene" (נצר = "branch"[59]) was used earlier in Israel by Jewish believers themselves (as well as others for that matter[60]) to designate members of their own Jewish movement[61] of believers in *Yeshua Ha Messiach* (יֵשׁוּעַ הַמָּשִׁיחַ = "Jesus Christ").[62] In regard to the original appellation, Dr. Ray Pritz writes—and he is, by the way, the best authority on early Jewish Christianity that I know of—that there was a heretical pre-Christian (or pre-Messianic Jewish) Jewish group with a similar name: "Nasaraioi." Known in antiquity by "Nasaraioi," "Nasarenoi," and/or "Nazorei"—from נסר or נשר, meaning "fallen," "fallen away," and/or "rebellious."[63] Understandably, owing to the similarity in the names, later Church Fathers sometimes inadvertently conflated the two groups.

Ancient Jewish believers in the non-Pauline sector of Jewish Christianity went by other names as well. Irenaeus (c. 130-200) explicitly referred to them as "The Poor"[64] ("The Poor" = אביון

---

[59] *Ibid.*, pp. 11-14.

[60] E.g., the Qumran sectaries.

[61] Cf., e.g., Matt. 2:23 and the Targum on Isa. 11:1 which says: "There shall come forth a king from the sons of Jesse, and a Messiah will grow from the sons of his sons" (Pritz, *Nazarene Jewish Christianity*, p. 13, n. 13). The point here is that the Targum uses "Messianic King" and "Branch" synonymously, as did the Qumran sectaries. (cf., e.g., 1Qsb V's application of Isa. 11:1, and Geza Vermes' introduction to "The Blessings" (1Qsb) in his *The Dead Sea Scrolls in English* [London: Penguin Books, 1990], p. 235). Pritz informs that Isa. 11:1 was also used in Midrash Lam. I, 51; Tanhuma (Buber) Vayehi 110; on 11:2 in Gen. R. III 4; XCIX 8; Midrash Ruth VII 2; on 11:4 in Midrash Ruth V 6; Midrash Song of Songs VI 10, 1; Shoher Tov 72; and on 11:10 in Gen. R. XCVIII 9; Tanhuma, Vayehi 10; Shoher Tov 21 (from Pritz, p. 13, n. 13, above).

[62] "Jesus Christ" is a transliteration of Ἰησοῦς Χριστός, which is the Greek form of Jesus' Hebrew name.

[63] Ray Pritz, *Nazarene Jewish Christianity*, p. 46.

[64] Cf., *Adv. haer.* I 26, 2; III 11,7; 21, 1; IV 33, 4: V 1, 3.

The Evolution of a Revolution

or πτωχός)—a pejorative expression that Eusebius parrots (see below). Epiphanius, in *panarion* 19,2,2, referred to a fringe group of Jewish believers as *Elxai* (חיל כסי = "hidden power") or "Elkasites." Additionally, and quite important for our purposes as well, he says, "They [i.e., the Iessaioi[65] (named afer Jesse, David's father) or the first Nazarenes] were "Jews [by birth]" and that, as such, "they dedicate[d] themselves to circumcision" (5,4). But these differed from most Jews; says Epiphanius: "[A]fter having heard the name of Jesus only, and having seen the divine signs performed by the hands of the apostles, they also believed in Jesus" (5,6).

Epiphanius goes on to again say that "Nazarenes," and *not* "Christians," was the first name for believers in Christ: "[E]veryone called the [first] Christians Nazarenes, as I said before." (6,1). Though these were the first, owing to their customs they were not acceptable to Epiphanius, who said: "they remained *wholly Jewish and nothing else*" (7,1). The Christian bishop was disturbed that these believers used "...not only the New Testament but also the Old, like the Jews"; additionally, says he: "They are not at all mindful of other things but [they] live according to the preaching of the Law as among Jews" (7,2). Having slighted them for this infraction, he nevertheless does realize that they are orthodox in that "They also accept the resurrection of the dead" and "They proclaim one God and his Son Jesus Christ" (7,3). In fact, says he, "Only

---

[65] Epiphanius says later: "[1,3] All Christians were called Nazarenes once. For a short time they were also given the name Iessians, before the disciples in Antioch began to be called Christians. [1,4] And they were called Iessaians because of Jesse, it seems to me, since David was from Jesse, and by lineage Mary was of the seed of David...." Significant is the fact that the text is divested of its literal meaning in order to make room for a spiritual priesthood—the Church. Epiphanius says: "[3,1] The throne of David and the royal seat are the priesthood in the holy church... He transferred the throne of David into the church, never to leave her. [4,6] Having sat down on the throne of the seed of David through Mary [the throne remains his] forever, and of his kingdon there shall be no end [Lk. 1:33]. Necessarily he also holds the order of the kingship. However, his kingdom is not from this earth, as he said to Pontius Pilate in the Gospel, 'My kingdom is not of this world.' [4,7] For that which was written was, to a degree, a figurative anticipation."

The Evolution of a Revolution

in this respect do they differ from Jews and Christians: with the Jews they do not agree because of their belief in Christ, [and] with the Christians because they are trained in the Law of circumcision, the Sabbath and other things" (7,5). Even though they hold to a proper Christology he still deems them heretical: "But these also have erred in boasting of circumcision, and such are still "under a curse" not being able to fulfill the Law" (8,1). *Their sole problem was that they desired to live and function as Jews, even after they had received Jesus*—something intolerable for Epiphanius: "For thus it is with every heresy, often trying to outdo each other in the matter prescribed concerning the keeping of the Sabbath and circumcision and other things, even though our Lord freely gave us a more perfect way" (8,5).

Epiphanius says that Nazarenes were headquartered in and around Judea: "This *heresy of the Nazarenes* exists in Beroea in the neighborhood of Coele Syria and the Decapolis in the region of Pella and in the Basanitis in the so-called Kokabe, Chochabe in Hebrew" (7,7); and then: "For *from there it took its beginning after the exodus from Jerusalem when all the disciples went to live in Pella because Christ had told them to leave Jerusalem and to go away since it would undergo a seige*. Because of this advice they lived in Perea after having moved to that place, as I said. There the Nazarene heresy had its beginning" (7,8).

Lastly, Epiphanius is also helpful in evidencing the deteriorating relationship between the Jewish believers in Jesus and those Jews who didn't believe in Jesus: "They are very much hated by the Jews" who pray in the synagogue for God to curse them: "Three times a day they say: 'May God curse the Nazarenes'" (9,2). What is the nature of the tension between the Nazarenes and the mainline Jewish community? Epiphanius says: "they are more hostile against them because they proclaim *as Jews* that Jesus is the Christ, which runs

-46-

The Evolution of a Revolution

counter to those who still are Jews who do not accept Jesus" (Italics mine. 9,3). Worthy of note is the fact that they wish to take their stand "as Jews." As we shall see, Epiphanius' testimony is corroborated by St. Jerome.

Jerome

Jerome (*Sophronius Eusebius Hieronymus*) served as a secretary to Pope Damascus in Rome; subsequently, he moved East where there was a greater premium placed on ascetic privations than in Rome. In 372 Jerome went to Antioch and in 375 he began his stay in the wilderness of Chalics ad Belum, during which time he learned Greek from, according to him, "a believing brother from among the Hebrews" (*Ep.* 125, 12 [*PL* 22, 1079]). He likewise learned Hebrew during this time—from a "believing brother" as well.

Jerome resided only 27 kilometers from Beroea, where, as was mentioned above, there was a Nazarene community. Even if he didn't have extended contact with them, Dr. Pritz feels that he was at least positioned to have known of them.[66] This is corroborated by Jerome in *de viris illustribus* 3:

> The Hebrew itself [of the original Gospel of Matthew] has been preserved until the present day in the library of Caesarea, which Pamphilius the martyr so diligently collected. From the Nazarenes who use this book in Beroea, a city in Syria, I also received the opportunity to copy it.

From the above we learn that Jerome had access to the Nazarenes and one of their documents: the Gospel of Matthew written in Hebrew. Jerome was a philologist; he greatly appreciated ancient languages and documents, and so he was very likely pleased to make use of their manuscript. His love for literature and language is attested by the work for which he is best known: the *Latin Vulgate*.[67]

---

[66] Ray Pritz, *Nazarene Jewish Christianity*, p. 51.

The Evolution of a Revolution

In around 404AD, Jerome wrote Augustine and said of the Nazarenes: "They believe in Christ, the Son of God, born of Mary the Virgin, and they say about him that he suffered under Pontius Pilate and rose again."[68] Worthy of note is the fact that, *according to Jerome, the Nazarenes reflect the orthodox Christology of the day.* He went on to inform Augustine that the they were *cursed by the Pharisees in the synagogues,* that they *keep the Law as well as embrace the faith,* and that they are *found in all the synagogues of the East among the Jews.*[69]

There are a number of references to the Nazarenes in Jerome's writings. In 398 Jerome wrote the following in his commentary on Matthew's Gospel: "Recently I read a certain Hebrew work, which a Hebrew person of the Nazarene sect offered me."[70] Additionally, in his commentary on Isaiah 8.14 Jerome said that the Nazarenes "accept Christ in such a way that they do not cease to observe the old law"—much as Epiphanious had attested; he likewise says in 8:20-21 how the Nazarenes opine: "God has given us the Law and the testimonies of Scripture." The above should suffice to buttress the case that *Jerome's Nazarenes lived in two worlds: evidently they believed in Jesus but lived as Jews nonetheless.* Worthy of note is the polemic between the Nazarenes and the rabbinic authorities, evidenced in Jeromes commentary on Isaiah 29:20-21:

> What we have understood to have been written about the devil and his angels, the Nazarenes believe to have been written against the Scribes and Pharisees....

It goes without saying that applying to the rabbinic teachers

---

[67] Elizabeth Livingston's *The Concise Oxford Dictionary of the Christian Church* (Oxford: Oxford University Press, 1987), p. 270.

[68] Ep. 112, 13 from Pritz, *Nazarene Jewish Christianity*, p. 53.

[69] *Ibid.*, p. 55.

[70] Matt. 27:9-10 (CC 77, 265) from Pritz, *Nazarene Jewish Christianity*, p. 56.

The Evolution of a Revolution

passages generally ascribed to the devil reflects on-going tensions between the Jewish and Messianic-Jewish communities.

Later, commenting on Isaiah 31:6-9, Jerome says that the Nazarenes urged other Jews to repent and join the Church:

> The Nazarenes understand this passage in this way: O sons of Israel, who deny the Son of God with a most vicious opinion, turn to him and his apostles... and the devil will fall before you....

If Jerome's statements are to be belived—and why wouldn't they be?—it is obvious that the Jewish community of believers in Jesus believed that the mainline Jewish religious authorities were infecting the Jewish populace with disbelief in Jesus' Messiahship, much as the devil infected and destroyed the human race. For this and other reasons, *it appears to me that the relationship between the Nazarene Jewish believers and the mainline Jewish community was rapidly deteriorating*—or had deteriorated—to say the least. *This deterioration can only be attributed to their stand for faith in Jesus as Israel's promised Messiah.* Mindful of this, they should have been commended by the Church at large—*but they weren't.*

In sum, *Jerome understood Nazarene Christology to be in line with the day's prevailing orthodoxy.* St. Jerome knew of both the existence of the Nazarene sect and their engagement in heated discourse with Jewish authorities, despite their adherence to the requirements promulgated in the Mosaic law.

Augustine

Let us now briefly consider St. Augustine, one of Western Christianity's most important churchmen.

According to Dr. Ray Pritz, Augustine, though he never knew the Nazarenes personally, was *instrumental in their being formally branded as heretics.* Says Pritz:

The Evolution of a Revolution

Augustine [bishop] of Hippo marks a decisive point in the history of the Church's view of the Nazarenes. While Epiphanius was the first to brand them as heretical, it was the authority of Augustine's acceptance of this judgment which seems to have fixed their fate and led to their final rejection by the Church.[71]

In his *treatise de baptismo contra Donastis*, St. Augustine says of the Nazarenes:

[J]ust as they persist to the present day who call themselves Nazarene Christians and circumcise the carnal foreskins in a Jewish way, are *born heretics* in that error into which Peter drifted and from which he was called back by Paul"[72] (VII 1,1).

From the above we learn that Nazarenes did exist into Augustine's day, that they practiced circumcision, and that St. Augustine castigated them for doing so: "heretics from birth" he calls them!

Regarding St. Augustine's feelings toward Jews in general, let the following suffice. In accordance with the spirit of the age, and in ways akin to his contemporaries,[73] St. Augustine

---

[71] Ray Pritz, *Nazarene Jewish Christianity*, p. 76.

[72] *Ibid*, pp. 76-77.

[73] Though St. Augstine's comments did service anti-Jewish sentiment, *in no way can he be credited with beginning it*. Note the following from St. John Chrysostom and then St. Jerome, for evidence of its prevalence: " The Jews are the most worthless of all men. They are lecherous, greedy, rapacious. They are perfidious murderers of Christ. They worship the devil, their religion is a sickness. The *Jews are the odious assassins of Christ* and for killing God there is no expiation possible, no indulgence or pardon. Christians may never cease vengeance, and the Jew must live in servitude forever. God always hated the Jews. It is incumbent upon all Christians to hate the Jews" (Italics mine; P. Grosser, and E. Halpern, *Anti-Semitism: Causes and Effects* [New York: Philosophical Library, Inc., 1983], p. 78. Also, consider St. Jerome, who says that Jews and their prayers were as *grunnitus suis et clamor asinorum* ("the grunting of a pig and the crying of donkeys") (James Charlesworth, *Jesus Within Judaism* [New York: Doubleday, 1988], p. 47). It's worth noting that St. Augustine never wrote anything of this sort about or against the Jews; specifically, he never

The Evolution of a Revolution

hung the death of Christ on the Jewish race as a whole. He *mistakenly* informed that "Jesus was crowned with Jewish thorns" (Bk. XVI 32)—in truth, Roman soldiers performed the deed according to the Gospels. There are other examples of his anti-Jewish bias as well. He is also on record as saying:

> The Jews held him, the Jews insulted him, the Jews bound him, they crowned him with thorns, dishonoured him by spitting upon him, they scourged him, they heaped abuse upon him, they hung him upon a tree, they pierced him with a lance.[74]

And also:

> *The true image of the Hebrew is Judas Iscariot,* who sells the Lord for silver. The Jew can never understand the Scriptures and will forever bear the guilt of the death of Jesus.[75]

According to St. Augustine, the Jews have a nature akin to Judas Iscariot! What is their destiny? Vanquished from God's economy, their lot is to suffer with the unrighteous—both now and in the future. God Himself would make them miserable in the next world; the Church would service Him by making them miserable in this one. *St. Augustine's anti-Judaism was real. His posture was part of a larger Christian tradition.* Christian anti-Judaism is a complicated subject; suffice it to say that *St. Augustine was not a friend to either Messianic Jewish believers in Jesus or Jewish non-believers in Jesus.*

---

accused them of killing God. It's for this reason that his anti-Judaism is quite mild as compared, let's say, to St. Jerome and St. John Chrysostom (Dr. William Babcock).

[74] Jules, I., *The Teaching of Contempt: Christian Roots of Anti-Semitism* (New York: McGraw Hill Book Company, 1965), p. 111; from Grosser, P., and Halpern, E., *Anti-Semitism: Causes and Effects*, pp. 79-80.

[75] Italics mine; Grosser, P., and Halpern, E., *Anti-Semitism: Causes and Effects*, p. 79.

The Evolution of a Revolution

Creedal Formulations as a Tool to "Weed Out" Jewish Believers Who Desired to Retain Their Jewish Identity

The following pathetic formulas were used, at the least, by the Church of Constantinople. As you will see, all Jewish believers in Jesus were required to publicly *denounce* their Jewish heritage and then *announce* that they had "seen the light" through the true Catholic Church.

Jewish believers in Jesus were forced to repeat the following as a confession of their faith:

> I renounce all customs, rites, legalisms, unleavened breads and sacrifices of lambs of the Hebrew, and all other feasts of the Hebrew, sacrifices, prayers, aspersions, purifications, sanctifications, and propitiations, and fasts and new moons, and Sabbaths, and superstitions, and hymns and chants and observances and synagogues, and the food and drink of the Hebrew; in one word, *I renounce absolutely everything Jewish, every law, rite and custom...*
>
> If I shall be found eating with the Jews, or feasting with them, or secretly conversing and condemning the Christian religion instead of openly confuting them and condemning their vain faith, then let the trembling of Cain and the leprosy of Gehazi cleave to me, as well as the anathema in the world to come, and may my soul be set down with Satan and the devils.[76]

Attached to the *Clementine Recognitions*[77] was an additional confession forced on the Jewish believers in Jesus. It expanded the one cited above:

> *I renounce the whole worship of the Hebrew,* circumcision, all its legalisms, unleavened bread,

---

[76] Italics mine. Assemani. Cod. lit. I, p. 105; gleaned from Schonfield's *The History of Jewish Christianity* (London: Duckworth Publishing, 1936), pp. 69-70.

[77] These writings, penned between 211-231 A.D., are no longer available in the Greek originals; however, they have survived in the Latin translations by Rufinus and in the Syriac.

The Evolution of a Revolution

Passover, the sacrificing of lambs, the feasts of Weeks, Jubilees, Trumpets, Atonement, Tabernacles and all other Hebrew feasts... *I absolutely renounce every custom and institution of the Jewish laws...*

Together with all these Jewish heresies and heresiarchs, deuteroses and givers thereof, I anathematize those who celebrate the feast of Mordecai [i.e., Purim]...

Together with the ancients, I anathematize the Chief Rabbis and new evil doctors of the Jews... Further, I evoke every curse and anathema on him whose coming is expected by the Jews as the Christ or Anointed, but is rather the Anti-Christ, and I renounce him and commit myself to the only true Christ and God. And I believe in the Father, the Son and the Holy Spirit, the Holy and consubstantial and Indivisible Trinity....[78]

Conclusion

In summary, we observe that a vibrant Messianic Jewish community flourished in Judea before Paul ever began his ministry in the Greco-Roman world. Both the Pauline and Judean communities placed a premium on charismatic giftings, evidenced by inspired preaching and supernatural healing. Owing to their extreme Jewish ethnocentrism, the Judean Messianic community *failed* as a force in the Greco-Roman world; however, owing to his innovations in cross-cultural communication—i.e., contextualization—Paul's enterprize was successful. As is always the case, *innovation causes confrontation!* The earliest Jewish and Gentile Christian communities were at odds with each other. Paul went to his grave trying to rectify the situation (cf., e.g., Acts 21: 17-26; 28:17-22).[79] Though Paul fought hard to bridge the gap between Messianic Judaism and the Greco-Roman "Christian" expressions, many who followed in his foot-steps had other

---

[78] Schonfield, *The History of Jewish Christianity*, pp. 71-72.

[79] Also, see Jouette M. Bassler's *God & Mammon: Asking for Money in the New Testament* (Nashville: Abingdon Press, 1991), pp. 89-116.

The Evolution of a Revolution

interests: it pleased them, for various reasons, to turn the rift into a gaping canyon.

Although Roman emperors had been somewhat tolerant of the Jews, the situation began to change with Constantine and the christianization of the empire.[80] Tragically, the Roman church became more and more determined to keep the Jews—*all* Jews—in a permanent state of misery and depravity.[81] What might have prompted various churchmen to be so vicious toward the Jews? Apparently, there was a strong element of *triumphalism* manifested by a Roman, Gentile church that was bent on proving that it—and *only* it—was fulfilling the God-ordained destiny of the people Israel. The Messianic Jews also had a legitimate claim to this. Due to the increasing authoritarian, monolithic consensus, they had to be either *absorbed* or *eliminated*.

More will be said about the relationship between the Christian and the Jewish communities later. Suffice it to say here that when Christianity became the Roman state religion, it seemed obvious to most that the Gentile Church was exalted to the status of "God's new Chosen People"—thus, triumphant over Jews. As the Christian religion was exalted, the synagogue was perceived solely as its ancient rival and thus denigrated. *Jewishness was despised.* The "faith"evolved and was given a facelift—or, faithlift—in the process. Sadly, the Jewish

---

[80] The following—an official letter from the Council of Nicea—evidences the trend: "[W]e desire, dearest brethren, to separate ourselves from the detestable company of the Jews... How can they be in the right, they who after the death of the Saviour, have no longer been led by reason but by wild violence as their delusion may urge them?... It would still be your duty not to tarnish your soul by communications with such wicked people [the Jews]... It is our duty not to have anything in common with the murderers of our Lord." (Eusebius, *Vita Const., Lib. iii*, 18-20; in *Nicean and Post-Nicean Fathers*, Vol. XIV [Grand Rapids: Eerdmans Publishing, 1979], p. 54). See also Robert Wilken, *John Chrysostom and the Jews: Rhetoric and Reality in the Late Fourth Century*, in *The Transformation of the Classical Heritage*, vol. 6, ed. Peter Brown (Berkeley: University of California Press, 1983), p. 53; also, Rosemary Radford-Ruether, in "Judaisn and Christianity: Two Fourth Century Religions," *Sciences Religeuses/Studies in Religion* 2:1-10, p. 186; both in Jacob Neusner, *Judaism and Christianity in the Age of Constantine*.

[81] Jacob Neusner, *Judaism and Christianity in the Age of Constantine*, p. 22.

The Evolution of a Revolution

message of Israel's promised Messiah was framed *exclusively* in non-Jewish terms and given a totally *non-Jewish* expression.

There is much to say about all of this, and the remainder of the book is dedicated to saying it. Ancient Christianity can be likened to a puzzle, of which this chapter, which swiftly covered hundreds of years, provided only the borders. In what follows, I will attempt to fill in some of the pieces to give my readers a clearer picture of the evolution of the revolution. This we'll do as we continue to consider Christianity's Judaistic, Hellenistic and Romanistic expressions.

The Evolution of a Revolution

II

Jewish Apocalyptic Expectation and New Testament Christian Eschatology

Introduction

This chapter's first section deals with Messianic-Judaism's major contribution to the world: the New Testament. The second is concerned with other ancient Jewish writings, from both the inter-testamental and New Testament periods, and considers ancient Jewish apocalyptic thought, language and literature. The third section, called "Meeting at the Crossroads," connects Jesus preaching to the Jewish eschatology in section two. The last section reflects on Pauline soteriology and eschatology. Paul is credited with "taking the Gospel to the Gentiles"—an appellation he earned owing to his penetration into the Hellenistic world; what he delivered, as we shall see, was still Israel's faith and message!

A. Good News from Ancient Jews
How the NT Story Evolved from an "Oral" to a "Written" Tradition

Jesus Christ—Christianity's founder—had gone to glory without ever writing a single book. During the first and earliest years of His Messianic movement's growth and expansion, the message was transmitted by an *oral tradition* only. Information about Jesus' life and teachings was passed on to new converts by those who were witness to the events first hand. By the end of the first century the last Apostle (John) had died and Jesus was no longer with them in the flesh; consequently, no longer could anyone make the claim that John did: "That that

The Evolution of a Revolution

we have heard, which we have seen with our eyes, which we have looked upon, and our hands have handled" (1 John 1:1)—*all* the original witnesses were dead.

Because of the passing of the first Apostles and as a result of the expansion of the Gospel beyond Israel's borders, various heterodoxical Greco-Roman faith communities began to feel pressed to produce some sort of official guide book to regulate their form of Christian faith and practice. False teachings surfaced claiming to be authentically Apostolic in origin and nature; owing to the resulting confusion, a standard (i.e., a "canon") was needed, to combat the rising tide of erroneous dogmatic assertions. Orthodoxy needed to be firmly established! To answer this need, various Church leaders began gathering all the fragments of Apostolic records in their respective regions[82] that might possibly be called into service[83]—thus the beginnings of a canon.

With minor doctrinal controversy on the one hand and the encroachment of major doctrinal heresy on the other, the ancient church Fathers felt pressed by the Spirit to sift through their ever-growing corpus of religious literature in order to ascertain the genuine inspired Apostolic documents from the pseudo-Apostolic pretenders. The following three tests, spelled out by Dr. Charles Ryrie, were employed by the church:[84]

> (1) There was the test of the *authority of the writer*—i.e., the book had to have either been written by an Apostle or have Apostolic authorization.
> (2) The books themselves had to give some

---

[82] And, of course, their teaching wasn't merely their own theological reflections; rather, it was/is the very Word of God, penned by inspiration from the Spirit of God.

[83] This regional activity produced various lists of "official" Christian holy writ. The Syrian Church's list differed some from, let's say, the Alexandrian list; both differed some from, let's say, the Roman list. It would be some years till the Church was sufficiently organized so that it could resolve the various conflicts. The present New Testament reflects the decision of the united Church on the "accepted books."

[84] Ryrie, C., *Ryrie Study Bible* (Chicago: Moody Press, 1978), p. 1853.

The Evolution of a Revolution

internal evidences of their unique character as inspired and thus authoritative.

(3) Lastly, the *verdict of the early Church* was very important—e.g., no text doubted by any large number of churches could be accepted into the canon.

Ancient Words & Modern Translations of those Words
Old Testament Hebrew

The late Dr. Edward Goodrick, professor of Greek and Bible at Multnomah School of the Bible, says that the Old Testament's language (primarily Hebrew, though others are included) is derived from a "Semitic mother-tongue" which birthed the following languages: Hebrew, Aramaic, Phoenician, Moabite, Ugaritic, Amorite, Akkadian, Ethiopic and Arabic.[85] The study of Old Testament language(s) has been enhanced by various modern archeological discoveries (e.g., the seventeen thousand tablets unearthed between 1974 and 1976 at Tell Mardikh, in northern Syria), evidencing the ancient usage of the above languages and thus enabling modern philologists to better understand the meanings of ancient Semitic idioms.

New Testament Greek

While the Old Testament's Hebrew language belonged to a Semitic linguistic family, the New Testament's Greek tongue belonged to an Indo-European language group. Antecedents to early Greek appear in Mycenaean Minoan documents (e.g., a hieroglyphic containing a "pre-Greek" syllabic script was found on both the Greek mainland and the island of Crete.[86]). The Mycenaean civilization, with its script, ended with the Dorian invasions of 1200 B.C.; later versions of "pre-Greek" appeared in Dorian, Ionian, Achaean and Aeolic forms. Eventually then, with the rise and spread of Greek culture, the Greek language—now having evolved into a classical, "Attic"

---

[85] Edward W. Goodrick, *Do It Yourself Hebrew and Greek* (Grand Rapids: Academie Books/ Zondervan; and Portland: Multnomah Press, 1980), p. 1:3.

[86] Larry Walker, "Biblical Languages," *The Origin of the Bible*, pp. 223-224.

The Evolution of a Revolution

form—became the international language of the Mediterranean basin. As a result of Alexander the Great's many military exploits, Greek culture and language spread beyond the Mediterranean, and a new form of Greek—one that assimilated some of the various regional dialects—was formed, called "Koine" (meaning "common") or "Hellenistic."[87] The New Testament was penned in this Koine Greek by Jewish-Christian writers who, says Dr. Larry Walker of the Mid-America Baptist Theological Seminary, "combined the directness of Hebrew thought with the precision of Greek expression."[88]

Modern Discoveries of Ancient Manuscripts

In the late nineteenth century, thousands of papyrus fragments were discovered in Oxyrhynchus, Egypt. Among the assorted documents were thirty-five copies of portions of the New Testament, known today by the title *Oxyrhynchus Papyri*. Purchased in Egypt a few years later, by Chester Beatty and the University of Michigan, was another collection called the *Chester Beatty Papyri*. The three manuscripts in this group contain large portions of the entire New Testament: from the second century there are portions of all four Gospels and Acts; from the late first and early second centuries come almost all of Paul's epistles and Hebrews; and, lastly, the Beatty collection contains a third century copy of the Revelation chapters 9-17. Purchased in the 1950's and 1960's, also in Egypt, the *Bodmer Papyri*, named after the owner M. Martin Bodmer, contains: a second century copy of almost all of John's gospel; a third century manuscript containing First and Second Peter and Jude; and a late second century copy of large parts of Luke 3 and John 15. Discovered by Dr. Constantin von Tischendorf in St. Catherine's Monastary, at the base of Mount Sinai, is a marvelous manuscript known as the *Codex Sinaiticus*, dated around 360. It contains the entire New

---

[87] *Ibid.*
[88] *Ibid.*, p. 227.

The Evolution of a Revolution

Testament, and it is one of the two oldest vellum manuscripts (i.e., treated animal hides) in existence today—the other being the *Codex Vaticanus*. The *Codex Vaticanus* is dated slightly earlier than the *Codex Sinaiticus*, at around 350. It's named after the Vatican library where it has been kept since 1481. This vellum manuscript contains both Old and New Testaments in Greek—excluding the Pastoral Epistles and Hebrews 9:15 to the end of Revelation. Other important manuscripts are: *Codex Alexandrius:* a fifth century manuscript containing nearly all of the present New Testament, with reliable witnesses to the General Epistles and Revelation, missing in the *Codex Vaticanus*; *Codex Washingtonianus:* a fifth century manuscript, currently housed in the Smithsonian Institute in Washington, containing all four of the Gospels; *Codex Bezae:* another fifth century manuscript, named after Theodor Beza its discoverer and containing text different from the previously mentioned manuscripts; and *Codex Ephraemi Rescriptus*, a palimpsest—i.e., a manuscript in which the original text was erased and written over to make room for another text.

There are in the ballpark some 6,000 extant NT manuscripts.[89] Mindful of this, given the fact that we can compare numerous copies, one may ask the following: Do we have an accurate record of apostlic/Messianic Jewish teaching or has the message been changed through the centuries? From what I understand, the New Testament we have is an accurate record of what the ancients wrote.[90]

Having briefly mentioned some major extant copies, let's now move on and consider the following important questions: (1) Where were these copies made? and (2) Who made them?

---

[89] See Hurtado, Larry W., "How The New Testament Came Down To Us," *Eerdmans' Handbook of the History of Christianity*, ed., Dowley, T. (Grand Rapids: Eerdmans, 1977), pp. 89-90, for a brief treatment of the manuscript finds.

[90] Dr. Philip Comfort opines: "not one fundamental Christian doctrine rests on a disputed reading" (See "Texts and Manuscripts of the New Testament," *The Origin of the Bible*, p. 182).

The Evolution of a Revolution

How New Testament Manuscripts Were Manufactured
Alexandrian Manuscripts

Alexandria, a prominent Egyptian metropolitan city, was the Mediterranean world's intellectual center. In conjunction with its being a philosophical/theological center, the city hosted scribes who were given to the production of Biblical manuscripts—e.g., the Septuagint.[91] The ancient Alexandrian library, renowned in antiquity, had a scriptorium staffed by trained philologists, grammarians and textual critics. Aristotle is said to have begun a tradition of classifying manuscripts; and Zenodotus is credited with the earliest attempt at ascertaining the vorlage (i.e., the text from which a translation was made) of various manuscript copies. An ancient textual critic, Zenodotus—the world's first librarian[92]— worked through discrepencies in manuscript copies, attempting to ascertain the text's original form. When satisfied that he had recovered the original, he produced an archetype which was deposited in the prestigious Alexandrian library. The Alexandrian Christian scribes and scholars, who followed,[93] employed well established Greek and Hebrew practices in plying their trade.

The point in all this is that textual reproduction developed into a science and an art form centuries prior to the Christian era. The earliest Christian scribes were Jewish converts to Christ, who naturally emulated the careful Jewish scribal traditions which were evolving over the centuries.

---

[91] The Septuagint (known in scholarly literature as the LXX) was an ancient Greek version of the Old Testament, penned in 250BC in Alexandria by Jewish scholars/scribes. The NT frequently quotes the Septuagint, evidencing that this Greek edition of the OT was preferred to Hebrew/Aramaic ones. This is only to be expected once we realize that, for the most part, people spoke Greek and not Hebrew.

[92] "Texts and Manuscripts of the New Testament," *The Origin of the Bible*, ed.. Philip Wesley Comfort (Wheaton: Tyndale House Publishers, 1992), p. 185.

[93] Eusebius recalls that a renowned catechetical school was established in Alexandria in the mid-second century AD. Clement was the school's head until persecution forced him to flee, after which Origen then served as the institution's headmaster.

The Evolution of a Revolution

Lucianic Manuscripts

Though Alexandria (Egypt) was host to the ancient world's most famous scriptorium, and one of the earliest famous Christian academies, it still was not the only city where people were engaged in religious studies and manuscript production. An Antiochian Christian named Lucian instigated a Greek rendering of the NT very much akin to some modern paraphrase versions. Lucian's text was produced just prior to the terrible Diocletian persecution (c. 303). After the scourge of those days, and when the Christian faith was recognized as the official religion of the empire, copies of the Christian faith's holy book were needed. Against this backdrop, says Dr. Philip Comfort, professor of New Testament at Wheaton College, Lucian's text—a casual edition *not* on par with the Alexandrian versions—"soon became the standard version [for the Eastern, Greek-speaking Church] and formed the basis for the Byzantine text."[94] Dr. Comfort explains that the Eastern "Orthodox" Church kept producing this inferior Greek version, based on the authority of a text known as the *Textus Receptus.*

The Textus Receptus (i.e., the "received text") is the primary source for the English King James Version. Though revered in some Fundamentalist camps,[95] neither the King James Version nor the Textus Receptus hold the high ground in a number of Evangelical circles,[96] owing to the discovery of

---

[94] "Texts and Manuscripts of the New Testament," *The Origin of the Bible*, p. 188

[95] It should be remembered that all English verisons of the Bible are but translations of a text that was written in other non-English languages. Those who argue that the Bible is God's Word—and *this writer desires to be included on that list*—are generally not arguing that a particular version of the Bible is the inspired inerrant Word, but that the original autographs themselves are inspired—the present versions being but translations of those original documents. Because a few see some versions as being the very Word of God, instead of it being but a translation of it, they have a certain bias against versions other than their preferred text (e.g., the K.J.V.). Isolated from the rest of Evangelical Christianity and smug in their intellectual ghettos, they go on reasoning that modern Evangelical scholarship is destructive and treacherous, and that its blasphemous to use versions other than their chosen translations.

manuscripts predating the Textus Receptus (see above).

My point here is simply that the ancient Alexandrian biblical manuscripts were made by professionals who held to extremely high standards of manuscript craftsmanship. It's for this reason that the Alexandrian-type Greek copies held sway in the early Christian church until the fourth century, after which they disappeared for centuries because of the growing popularity of Latin and St. Jerome's Latin translation.

The Church's Authoritative Canon
Introduction

In "The Uses of Holy Scripture" Dr. Maurice Wiles asserted that in ancient preliterate society books themselves, apart from their contents, contained an "aura of rarity and mystery."[97] Prior to the advent of the printing press, books were indeed quite rare. Claiming to be written by gods or about gods, it is easy to see how these rare books would contain a certain amount of awe and mystery. Professor Wiles cited Dr. A. D. Nock, who declared: "[T]hroughout the imperial period one of the conspicuous features of intellectual life was a readiness to accept statements [simply] because they were in books."[98] To this Professor Delwin Brown added, leaning on Dr. Arendt, that our concept of authority is "[Greco-]Roman in origin,"[99] and that, as such, it rests on documents alleged to having been written by or about the figures who "laid the foundations."[100]

---

[96] Some argue that the reverence for the KJV gets in the way of good scholarship. Dr. Henry Alford, in his preface for the *Greek New Testament*, said (of the Textus Receptus) that he labored for the "demolition of the unworthy and pedantic reverence for the received text, which stood in the way of all chance of discovering the genuine Word of God" (p. 190). Frankly, I believe that irreverence like this is quite harmful. It comes, most likely, as a result of extreme frustration—understandable but not justifiable.

[97] *Explorations in Theology* 4, ed. Maurice Wiles (SCM, 1979), p. 74.

[98] *Ibid.*, p. 76.

[99] "Struggle till Daybreak: On the Nature of Authority in Theology," in *The Journal of Religion*, Vol. 65 (Nu. 1, Jan. 1985), p. 20.

[100] *Ibid.*, pp. 20-21; extracted from Hannah Arendt "What Was Authority?" in *Authority*, ed. Carl. J. Friedrich (Cambridge: Harvard University Press, 1958), pp.

The Evolution of a Revolution

The New Testament has traditionally been vested with certain authority because of the correct notion that the documents were Apostolic in origin. The outgrowth of all this in Christian circles was the development of a formal doctrine of the NT's canonical authority. The word "canon" comes from the Greek κανών (*kanon*), a word that is similar in Hebrew, קָנֶה (*kaneh*) and means a "reed, a measuring rod, or a ruler." The expression "rule of faith" is derived from "canon," and speaks of its *authoritas canonica sive normata* (canonical and normative authority). In what follows, we'll look more closely at authority.

Authority and Biblical Authority

The expression "authority," as it relates to "religious authority" and was used by ancient believers, has meanings that are both manifold and ambiguous. In the OT we find the following words used to reflect authority: רבה (*rabbah*= "to be great," cf., Pro. 29:2) and תקף (*tokeph* = "authority," cf., Esth. 9:29). In the NT ἐξουσία is used to denote authority (*exousia* = "it is lawful") as well as ἐξουσιάζω (*exousiazo*) meaning the "exercise of [that] power."[101] κατεξουσιάζω (*katexousiazo*) has an object in view, meaning the "exercise of authority upon," as does ἐπιταγή (*epitage*) which means "to order upon," "to command." To dominate, or to exercise authority on one's own account, is reflected by αὐθεντέω (*authenteo*). ὑπεροχή (*hyperoche*) was also used in koine Greek to denote "preeminence" or "superiority," and refers to a high position, e.g., a magistrate,[102] as does δυνάστης (*dunastes*).[103]

The expression "authority," as it relates to "Biblical[104]

81-112.

[101] E.g. Matt. 9:6; 21:23; 2 Cor. 10:8.

[102] E.g. Rom. 13:1-3; Lk. 12:11; Tit. 3:1.

[103] Culled from *The International Standard Bible Encyclopaedia*, Vol. I (Grand Rapids: Eerdmans, 1984), pp. 333-335; and *Vine's Expository Dictionary of New Testament Words* (Mc Lean, Va.: Mac Donald Publishing, n.d.), pp. 91-92.

[104] Βιβλία (*Biblia*): "Book." It is worth noting that other religions—e.g., Zoroastrian, Hindu, Buddhist and Mohammedan—also have sacred writings

authority" and was used by post-OT/NT Latin churchmen, comes—like the above—replete with a host of complexities. Dr. Richard A. Muller, of the Fuller Theological Seminary, is helpful in sorting out some of the particulars. He informs that *Authoritas* speaks of power at work that derives from its author (*auctor*). Churchmen used *authoritas divina duplex* to speak of two types of Christian authority—distinct yet related: (1) *authoritas rerum* referred to the authority of scriptural things (i.e., *substantia doctrinae* or "the substance of doctrine"); whereas (2) *authoritas verborum* (i.e., the "authority of the words of Scripture") spoke of the written word, and was derived from the *accidens scriptionis* (the accident of writing).[105] The "authority of Scripture" (*authoritas Scripturae*) rested on a doctrine of "inspiration" (*inspirato*), which postulated that Scripture was θεόπνευστος (*theopneustos* or "God breathed"[106]). Against this backdrop, the Protestant scholastics perceived the Bible as *principium cognoscendi et ebiectum formale fidei ac theologiae revelatae* ("The foundation of knowing and formal object of faith and revealed theology") as well as *in rebus fidei ac morum* ("The canon or norm, resting on inspiration, for all discernment of truth and falsehood in matters of faith and morals"). Owing to its assumed divine origin, Scripture was graced with a doctrine of *infallibilitas* ("infallibility") and was deemed to possess *veritas assertionum sine admixtis erroribus* ("truth without admixture of error") and was thus referred to as the *norma normans non normata* (i.e., the norm for matters of faith).[107]

---

refered to, by some, as their "Bible" (*The International Standard Biblical Encyclopaedia*, Vol. I, [Grand Rapids: Eerdmans, 1984], p. 460).

[105] Richard A. Muller, *Dictionary of Latin and Greek Theological Terms* (Grand Rapids: Eerdmans, 1989), p. 51.

[106] 2 Tim. 3:16 is the usual reference used to support the assertion.

[107] Cf., Haight, R., *The Dynamics of Theology* (New York: Paulist Press, 1990), p. 89; and Muller, R., *Dictionary of Latin and Greek Theological Terms* (Grand Rapids: Baker Book House, 1985), p. 203.

The Evolution of a Revolution

Theology and Biblical Theology

In modern Hebrew, "theology" is known by תאולוגיה (a mere transliteration) and is referred to as תורה האלהות, meaning "God's teaching."[108] In English the word "theology" comes from the Greek θεός (God) and λόγος (word or reason), and conveys the same notion. For centuries theology was understood as the "science of things divine."[109] "Holy Scripture" is generally referred to, in Judaism, as the תנך[110] and/or the תורה (which means "teaching," or "Law").[111] In NT Greek, Scripture is called γραφή and is used therein to refer to sacred writings.[112] Historically there has been an inextricable relationship between Christian theology and Christian Scripture. Christian theology derived its authority because, among other things, it reflected on NT Sacred Writ, which was Messianic-Jewish/Apostolic teaching in written form.

Traditional communities have construed Bible-based Christian theology as *Theologia a Deo docetur, Deum docet, et ad Deum ducit* (from Thomas Aquinas, meaning "Theology is taught *by God,* teaches *of God* and leads *to God*"). Christian Theology has been generally described as *theologia as sermo vel ratio de Deo* (i.e., a word or *rational discourse* concerning God, and therefore as human wisdom or knowledge concerning God).[113] The classical Christian position held that proper theology was *theologia supernaturalis sive revelata*

---

[108] R. Alcalay, *The Complete English-Hebrew Dictionary*, Vol. II (Israel: Chemed Books, 1990), p. 3787.

[109] *Encyclopaedia Judaica*, Vol. 15 (Jerusalem: Keter Publishing, 1971), p. 1103. Here theology is also referred to as "a sustained *rational* discourse on God" (italics mine), very much akin to the Christian understanding above.

[110] The word "Tanach" (תנך) is an acronym created from the first letter of each of the following Hebrew words: *Torah* (תורה), *Neviim* (נביאים) and *Ketuvim* (כתובים)—or *Law, Prophets and Writings*.

[111] Ben Isaacson, *Dictionary of the Jewish Religion* (Englewood: Bantam Books, 1979), p. 165.

[112] *Vines Expository Dictionairy of New Testament Words*, pp. 1011-1012.

[113] Italics mine. Richard A Muller, *Dictionary of Latin and Greek Theological Terms* (Grand Rapids: Baker Book House, 1985), p. 298. This is the primary source for muct of what follows in Latin.

The Evolution of a Revolution

(theology revealed from God, supernaturally, and thus inaccessible to unaided human reason[114]). It's this last notion that needs correction: *theology must be aided by human reason.*

Summary

To begin my summary, I'll refer to Dr. Russell Spittler, a professor at Fuller Theological Seminary, who said:

> I discovered that the Scripture had not dropped from heaven as a sacred meteor that arrived intact. I learned (and should have known much earlier) that the books of the Bible grew from the soil of fervent Christian activity in a real though long-ago world, [and] that [the] literature is a centrifugal spin-off of history.[115]

I agree with Professor Spittler, though I would add that *NT* literature, itself, is a centrifugal spin-off of *Jewish* history. The NT collection's being collected, finally, is the result of Christian history—thus "Christian activity"; but the documents themselves can only be fully appreciated when they are considered in their Jewish *Sitz im Leben* (i.e., their "situation in life"—a theological expression for "context").

Sadly, given that the New Testament's primary interpreters were non-Jewish and even anti-Jewish, many never got a hold of that "context." Latin churchmen, hundreds of years removed from the New Testament period, thus out of touch with the NT's Jewish ethos (see below), lost sight of the Christian connection to the nation and people of Israel. The

---

[114] Schubert Ogden does not believe this to be the case (cf. "What is Theology?," *On Theology* [San Francisco: Harper & Row, 1986] pp. 1-21); he says, "[T]heology without faith is still theology, and quite possibly *good theology* at that" (Italics mine. *Ibid.*, p. 19).

[115] Russell Spittler, "Scripture and the Theological Enterprise," in *The Use of the Bible in Theology: Evangelical Options*, ed. Robert K. Johnston (Atlanta: John Knox Press, 1985), p. 63.

The Evolution of a Revolution

following two sections should help us recover that "connection."

B. New Testament Eschatology and Jewish Jewish Apocalyptic Expectation
Introduction

I anticipate that this section will, at first, likely be a bit disorienting for some. Why? *Herein I will demonstrate that the New Testament's kerygmatic and eschatological language betrays a non-Christian, Jewish source.* This will strike some as strange and possibly even heretical. Before moving in this direction, however, and by way of introduction, I believe that a word is called for about the reason for, and value in, such an enterprise, beginning with an explanation of the nature and origin of Jewish apocalyptic literature.

Apocalyptic literature became popular in and around Judea long before John ever put pen to paper to write the famous book entitled the Revelation.[116] Many ancient Jews were frustrated by the Roman domination of Judea, and longed for the day when the Messiah would come and wrest them free from the Roman yoke. Of course, as we know, the dream was *not* realized, for the Romans eventually destroyed both the Jewish nation and the Jewish Temple. Owing to their inability to see the realization of the long-awaited Messianic era, many Jews took refuge from their harsh world in the fantastic stories of assorted charismatic "seers"—folk who claimed to have had special inspired visions and insights on *how* and *when* the Davidic kingdom would finally arrive to free the Hebrews from Gentile domination and establish lasting world peace. Their eschatological scenarios are preserved in assorted pseudepigraphical works, many of which have been translated into English. Herein, as I'd said, we will concern ourselves with some aspects of this ancient apocalyptic genre,

---

[116] E. Isaac, "1 (Ethiopic Apocalypse of) Enoch" in the *The Old Testament Pseudepigrapha*, Vol. I., ed. James H. Charlesworth (Garden City: Doubleday & Company, Inc., 1983), p. 9.

The Evolution of a Revolution

specifically the pseudepigraphical works of 1 Enoch, 4 Ezra, and the Apocalypse of Baruch.

Dr. George W, Macrae, a professor at Harvard University, believes that pseudepigraphical literature augments New Testament studies, because students are then enabled to better understand ancient Judaic eschatological idioms. He says: We need to know "as much [as we can] about the [New Testament] Biblical world in all of its facets."[117] Of course, apocryphal and pseudepigraphical literature—from the Gnostic Nag Ham-madi codices to the Dead Sea Scrolls, to various extracts preserved solely in Christian Syriac, Greek, Ethiopic and Latin translations—satisfy this need quite nicely. Agreeing with Dr. Macrae on this score, I am convinced that New Testament exegetes will be well served by becoming acquainted with the non-canonical books, both for their own sake as well as for the light they shed on the ancient New Testament *world* and *vocabulary*.[118]

On the surface of it, the kind of inquiry suggested here does *seem* to threaten the integrity of the New Testament. Why? A cursory examination of the period's literature evidences the fact that *the New Testament's eschatological language isn't at all unique to the New Testament.* Understandably, some may find this troubling—at first. It's not at all unreasonable, or unexpected, that one would ask the following two questions: (1) Is not the historical-critical work being suggested here one of the "Liberal" disciplines that tends to denigrate Holy Writ?; and (2) Would not such a study tend to injure the "inspired" status of the New Testament?[119] Concerning "Historical Criticism" and the question posed regarding it—i.e., Is it harmful?—let me state the following: historical criticism may

---

[117] *The Old Testament Pseudepigrapha*, Vol. I., p. ix.

[118] On this score, I'm agreeing with the late Oxford luminary, Dr. W. Sanday, in G. H. Box's *The Ezra Apocalypse* (London: Sir Isaac Pitman & Sons, 1912), p. 5.

[119] The answer to that depends on who is using historical criticism, and what sort of presuppositions they hold.

The Evolution of a Revolution

be responsibly employed to service New Testament studies[120]: though it may be employed as a *servant* of the New Testament, never should it be used as a *master* of the sacred Text.[121] Again, I believe that there is value *if* em-ployed properly. In fact, most Evangelical exegetes work with the historical backgrounds of sacred Holy Writ and, in fact, see doing so as a *necessary prerequisite to proper exegesis.*[122]

What will one discover in the following pages? Our cursory examination of pseudepigraphical literature will turn up evidence that NT concepts such as "Son of Man," "tribulation period," "heaven," "hell," "judgment day," "new heaven" and "new earth," etc., were in *common use* amongst the Jews in Jesus' day. Because most New Testament students first confront these expressions in the New Testament, many naturally assume that they are the exclusive property of the New Testament. Wrong! This *improper* misunderstanding will need to give way to a better understanding; for, as we shall clearly see, these Judaic expressions were part of the Jewish vocabulary *outside* of the community of Jesus' immediate followers. How can this be? Simply put, they spring from a *common source* that ancient Jews and then ancient Jesus followers—themselves Jews too, for the most part—held in common: the Old Testament.

Ancient Jews, like all people, developed a vocabulary through which they articulated their understanding of their Bible, their world, and the way they felt the two went together.[123] Jesus came and spoke to Jewish people using an

---

[120] In fact, no modern Conservative Evangelical theologian ignores it (cf., e.g. *The Use of the Bible in Theology: Evangelical Options,* ed. Robert K. Johnston (Atlanta: John Knox Press, 1985).

[121] Basically, it can be said that this is the fundamental error of those in the "Liberal" camp.

[122] Cf., e.g.,*The Use of the Bible in Theology: Evangelical Options,* above.

[123] Twentieth century Evangelicals have done the same. Modern believers have likewise developed colloquialisms to reflect present stances on eschatology (e.g., "Rapture," "Dispensationalism"), and ecclesiology (e.g., "Five-Fold Ministry," "Priesthood of Believers") to name but a few. Additionally our vocabulary is full of inherited "Christian" theological terms (e.g., "Trinity") that we use with relative ease. Though never used in the Bible, these terms have worked their

existing nomenclature, a language that came replete with maxims and mental images reflecting an underlying Biblical theology. In His parabolic sayings, Jesus made use of exisiting vocabulary for His ethical instructions to His Judean followers.[124] Likewise, He employed existing Jewish eschatological language—an articulation of their understanding of events predicted in the Bible—to speak of the coming Kingdom, and beyond. It's only to be expected that the New Testament would contain many prevailing Judaic expressions—hebraisms. Simply put, *the non-canonical pseudepigraphical genre enables us to better understand that idiom*; this, in turn, aids students in New Testament studies by making the language of both Jesus' and Paul's era more intelligible to both modern Christian and Jewish readers.

First (Ethiopic Apocalypse of) Enoch
Introduction

The book of 1 Enoch originated in Judea and was in use at Qumran—the Essene community where the *Dead Sea Scrolls* were penned—prior to the Christian era.[125] 1 Enoch comes down from antiquity in Aramaic, Ethiopic, Greek and Latin forms; but there's a cogent argument that these were translated originally from a Hebrew vorlage. In any event, as was mentioned, the book does come from a Judaic milieu; and, owing to its popularity in early Jewish circles—as evidenced by its usage in Baruch, Ezra and the New Testament[126] (see below)—it's deemed worthy of our consideration. Likewise, this Jewish book

---

way into our vocabulary to express our understanding of the Bible in much the same way as the ancients developed vocabulary to articulate their understanding of Sacred Writ.

[124] On this score, I'm pleased to recommend Dr. Brad Young's work in the field. In particular, I found *The Jewish Background to the Lord's Prayer* (Dayton: Center for Judeo-Christian Studies, 1984) to be quite helpful, as well as *Jesus and His Jewish Parables* (New York: Paulist Press, 1989).

[125] E. Isaac, 1 (Ethiopic Apocalypse of) Enoch, in *The Old Testament Pseudepigrapha*, Vol. I, p. 8.

[126] I see the New Testament as a Jewish source.

The Evolution of a Revolution

was *highly regarded* by many of the Church Fathers, owing to the many points of contact between it and the New Testament.

Here, I am primarily concerned with introducing my readers to *Enoch's understanding of the termination of the present age and the inauguration of the next one.* Enoch's vocabulary is worth noting. Through various visions and dialogues that he allegedly has been privileged to have with heavenly beings, an eschatological picture emerges that is very much akin to the New Testament's—even though the pseudonymous work in question pre-dates the Christian era *by over a century.* Saving the consideration of its relationship to the New Testament till later, let's first attend to the story.

In what follows immediately, I will briefly reconstruct 1 Enoch's eschatological scenario(s). Having done so, I will then examine various pericopes from 1 Enoch.

Reconstruction of the Eschatology in 1 Enoch
Arrangement of Material

In the latter days, earth dwellers will be thrust into a period of tribulation. This horrific period will terminate at the Messiah's advent (1 Enoch 91:5-17). The natural order will be thrown out of kilter, and there will be an apparent change of the times and seasons (1 Enoch 80:2-8). At the beckoning of angels, the kings of the earth will be gathered together for battle; finally they will be destroyed (1 Enoch 56:5-8) by the Son of Man (i.e., the Messiah), who is instrumental in both provoking and terminating the final conflict (1 Enoch 46:1-5).

God will visit Mount Zion with his holy army, and rescue the "chosen" people from the clutches of the wicked (1 Enoch 1:1-9). He will proceed to give to both the righteous and the wicked their just rewards: life and death eternal (1 Enoch 62:1-14; 103:4-8). With the overthrow of the dark and oppressive forces, power will be transferred to the meek, who will then go on to inherit the earth (1 Enoch 5:7; 38:3-5). The righteous will rejoice, while the wicked writhe in agony; for they will be

The Evolution of a Revolution

condemned along with the fallen angels (1 Enoch 69:26-29). In sum, the wicked will be condemned; but, happily, the earth will be rejuvenated and a just society will be ordered for the righteous (1 Enoch 10:13-11:2).

The "Head of Days" (God) will sit on his throne and the judgement books will be opened (1 Enoch 47:3) by him who will judge even the secrets of man's heart (1 Enoch 49:4). Those who spoke evil against God will be thrust into hell (1 Enoch 27:2). Fallen angels will be sent to the abyss (1 Enoch 18:9-19:3): Enoch is specifically informed that they will be chained and carted off to destruction (1 Enoch 54:1-6; 56:1), that it's a place of never ending torment (1 Enoch 21:7-10), and that it's an eternal oven (1 Enoch 98:3).

Eternal life will be granted to the just (1 Enoch 71:13-17); and they, being those who have their names inscribed in the Book of Life, will shine like the stars (1 Enoch 58:2-3; 104:1-4).

There will be a new heaven and a new earth (1 Enoch 45:3-6). Man and animal alike will rejoice in the regeneration that attends the Messianic era (1 Enoch 51:4-5). The nations of the world will pay homage to the victorious Son of Man during His ministration on the rejuvenated planet (1 Enoch 48:1-10).

Throngs will gather around the enthroned Lord and forever sing His praises (1 Enoch 14:16-23; 39:10-13). There will be good reason to offer up continual, jubilant praise to the Lord; for planted in Paradise is a tree with a fragrance that causes sorrow and sickness to cease (1 Enoch 25:3-7): in short, members of the regenerated commonwealth will enjoy a cessation of all evils—finally, genuine felicity!

A Closer Look at 1 Enoch

Having outlined what I believe to be the basic flow of events in Enoch's eschatology, it remains to be seen whether or not my understanding can be borne out by a cursory reading of the text. Owing to the fact that the above mentioned themes are

The Evolution of a Revolution

repeated a number of times and in various contexts, I took the liberty of *not* producing the pericopes in the order that they appear in 1 Enoch.[127] Instead, I felt that a *thematic approach*—as reflected above and outlined below—would be more helpful. It remains for my readers to determine whether or not they feel my heuristic model is helpful.

An Introduction to the General Scheme

Enoch envisions that the planet earth will fall into a tumultuous period of great tribulation. This period will come to an end with the advent of the Messiah (91:5-17).

> [I] know that a condition of oppression will grow strong on the earth, and great punishment will be completed over the earth... and again injustice will be repeated... And then injustice and sin and reviling and oppression and all the deeds will increase, and falling-off and reviling and uncleanness will increase; there will be a great punishment from heaven upon them all, and the holy Lord will come forth in anger, and with punishment, that he may pass judgement on the earth. And in those days oppression will be cut off from its roots... the roots of injustice will be cut off, and the sinners will be destroyed with the sword, and the roots of the revilers will be cut off in every place... And the first heaven will pass away and cease, and a new heaven will appear, and all the powers of heaven will shine to eternity... there will be many weeks without number, to eternity, in goodness and in justice, and sin will not be mentioned from that time on to eternity.

During the last days—i.e., during the period of dire tribulation—there will be an apparent changing of the times

---

[127] For those interested, here is their order of appearance in the text: 1:1-9; 5:7; 10:13-11:2; 14:16-23; 18:9-19:3; 21:7-10; 25:3-7; 27:2; 38:3-5; 39:10-13; 45:3-6; 46:1-5; 47:3; 48:1-10; 49:4; 51:4-5; 54:1-6; 56:1-8; 58:2-3; 60:7; 24; 62:1-14; 69:26-29; 71:13-17; 80:2-8; 91:5-17; 98:3; 103:4-8; 104: 1-4.

The Evolution of a Revolution

and seasons (80:2-8).

> And in the days of the sinners the years will be shortened.. the fruit of the earth will be tardy... the moon will change her order and will not appear in her time... And many leaders of the stars of command will err, and they will change their paths and deeds, and those subject to them will not appear on time....

Wars are decreed! At the beckoning of angels, the kings of the earth will be gathered together for battle; finally they will be utterly destroyed (56:5-8) by the Son of Man (i.e., the Messiah), who will visit the earth for that very purpose (46:1-5).

> And in those days the angels will assemble, and turn their heads toward the east, toward the people of Parthia and Media, in order to excite the kings, and that a disturbance come over them from off their thrones, that they come forth from their resting places like lions, and like hungry wolves amidst their flocks. And they will ascend and step upon the land of their chosen, and the land of his [i.e., God's] chosen will be before them [and they will be defeated]... And in those days [after the battle] the mouth of sheol will be opened, and they will sink into it; and their destruction, Sheol, will devour the sinners from the presence of the chosen.

And,

> And there I saw one who had a head of days [i.e., was old], and his head was white like wool; and with him was a second whose countenance was like the appearance of man... And I asked one of the angels, who went with me, and who showed me all the secrets, concerning this son of man, who he was

The Evolution of a Revolution

and whence he was, and why he goes with the Head of days? And he answered and said unto me: "This is the Son of man, who has justice, and justice dwells with him, and all the treasuries of secrets he reveals, because the Lord of the spirits has chosen him, and his portion overcomes all things before the Lord of the spirits in rectitude to eternity. And this Son of man, whom thou hast seen, will rouse the kings and mighty from their couches, and the strong from their thrones, and will loose the bands of the strong, and will break the teeth of the sinners. And he will expel the kings from their thrones and from their kingdoms, because they do not exalt him and praise him, and do not acknowledge humbly whence the kingdom was given to them.

God will visit his Mount with his army, and He'll rescue the "chosen" people from the clutches of the wicked (1:2-9).

[T]he Holy and Great One, will come from his abode, the God of the world. And from there he will step on Mount Sinai, and appear with his hosts, and appear in the strength of his power from heaven... And the earth will be submerged, and everything that is on the earth will be destroyed, and there will be a judgment upon everything, and upon all the just. But to the just he will give peace, and will protect the chosen, and mercy will abide over them, and they will all be God's and will be prosperous and blessed, and the light of God will shine for them. And behold, he comes with myriads of the holy to pass judgement uon them, and will destroy the impious, and will call to account all flesh for everything the sinners and the impious have done and committed against him.

He will then give to both the righteous and the wicked their just rewards: life and death eternal (62:1-14; 103:4-8).

The Evolution of a Revolution

> Open your eyes, and lift up your horns, if ye are able to recognise the Chosen One. And the Lord of the spirits sat on the throne of his glory... and the word of his mouth slew all the sinners and all the impious, and they were destroyed before his face... [The wicked] will look one upon another, and will tremble and caste down their countenances, and pain will seize them, when they see this Son of woman sitting on the throne of his glory... For formerly the Son of man was hidden, and the Most High preserved him before his power, and has revealed him to his chosen. And all the powerful kings and exalted and they who rule the earth will fall before him upon their faces, and will worship and will hope in this Son of man, and will petition him and ask him for mercy [but to no avail.]... And the angels of punishment will receive them to take vengeance on them, because they abused his children, his chosen... the sword of the Lord of the spirit is drunk with them... [Of the righteous] ...the Lord of the spirits will dwell over them, and they will dwell with this Son of man, and will eat and lie down and rise again with him to all eternity.

And,

> And your souls will live, ye who have died in justice, and your spirits will rejoice and be glad, and their remembrance will be before the face of the Great One to all the generations of eternity... [And of the wicked] Do you know that their souls will be caused to descend into Sheol, and it will be ill with them, and their trouble great. And in darkness and in toils and in a burning flame their spirits will burn at the great judgment; and a great judgment will be for all generations to eternity.

With the overthrow of the dark and oppressive forces,

The Evolution of a Revolution

power will be transferred to the meek, who will then go on to inherit the earth (5:7; 38:3-5).

> [F]or the chosen there will be light and joy and peace, and they will inherit the earth, but for you the impious there will be a curse.

And,

> And when the secrets of the just shall be revealed, then the sinners will be judged, and the impious will be expelled from the presence of the just and chosen. And from that time those who hold the earth will not be powerful and exalted, nor will they be able to behold the face of the just, for the light of the lord of the spirits is seen on the face of the just and chosen. And the mighty kings will perish at that time, and will be given over into the hands of the just and holy.

The righteous will rejoice; the wicked writhe in agony, for they will be condemned along with the fallen angels (69:26-29).

> And there was great joy among them, and they blessed and honored and exalted, because the name of the Son of man had been revealed to them... [Sitting upon his throne] he [i.e., the Son of man] causes to disappear and to be destroyed the sinners from the face of the earth. They shall be bound with chains and shall be imprisoned in the assemblage-place of destruction....

In sum, the wicked will be condemned; happily, a just society will be ordered upon a rejuvinated earth (10:13-11:2).

> And in those days they will be led to the abyss of fire, in torture and in prison they will be locked for all eternity... they will be burned together from

now on to the end of all generations... all wicked deeds shall cease, and the plant of justice and righteousness shall appear... justice and righteouness will be planted in joy forever. Then all the just will bend the knee, and they will remain alive till they beget a thousand children, and they will complete all their days of their youth and their sabbath in peace. And in those days the whole earth will be worked in justice, and will all be planted with trees, and will be full of blessings. And all the trees of desire will be planted on it, and vines will be planted on it; the vine planted on it will bear fruit in abundance. And all the seed sown on it in one measure will bear ten thousand, and one measure of olives will make ten presses of oil. And cleanse thou the earth of all oppression and injustice and all sin and all wickedness and all uncleanness which are produced on the earth: eradicate them from the earth. And the children of men shall become just, and all the nations shall worship me as God, and bless and all will worship me. And the earth will be cleansed of all corruption and all sin and all punishment and all torment, and I will never again send a flood upon it, from generation to generation, to eternity. "And in those days I will open the storerooms of blessings which are in heaven, in order to bring them down upon the earth, upon the deeds and labor of the children of men. Peace and rectitude will become associates in all days of the world, and in all generations of the world."

Eternal Condemnation for the Wicked and Eternal Bliss for the Righteous

The Head of Days (God) will sit on his throne and the judgment books will be opened (47:3) by him who will judge even the secrets of man's heart (49:4).

I saw the Head of days, as he sat upon the throne of

The Evolution of a Revolution

his glory, and the books of the living were opened before him, and his whole host, which is in high heaven and around him, stood before him.

And,

And he will judge the secrets, and no one will be able to speak a vain word before him, because he is the Chosen One before the Lord of the spirits, according to his will.

Those who blaspheme will be thrust into hell (27:2).

[Said the angel Uriel, to Enoch:] "This cursed valley is for those who will be cursed for eternity, and here will be assembled all those who have spoken with their mouths unseemly words against God...; here they will be assembled, and here will be their judgment...."

Fallen angels will be sent to the abyss (18:9-19:3).

And I saw a burning fire which was in all the hills. And there I saw a place, beyond the great earth... And I saw a great abyss in the earth, with columns of heavenly fire... The angel said: "This is the place of consumation of heaven and earth; it is a prison for the stars of heaven, and for the host of heaven... they who have transgressed the command of God... he was enraged at them, and bound them till the time of the consummation of their sins in the year of mystery." And Uriel said to me: "Here will stand the souls of those angels who have united themselves with women, and having assumed many different forms, have contaminated mankind, and have led them astray so that they brought offerings to demons as to gods, namely on the day when the great judgment, on which they will be judged, shall be consummated. And their

The Evolution of a Revolution

> women having led astray the angels of heaven, will be like their friends." And I, Enoch, alone saw this vision, the ends of all; and no man has seen them as I have seen them.

Enoch is specifically informed that evil angels will be chained and carted off to destruction (54:1-6; 56:1).

> And I looked and turned toward another side of the earth, and I saw there a deep valley with a burning fire. And they brought the kings and the powerful and put them into the deep valley. And there my eyes saw how they make instruments for them, iron chains of immense weight. And I asked the angel of peace, who went with me, saying: "These chain instruments, for whom have they been prepared?" And he said to me: "These have been prepared for the hosts of Azazel, to imprison them and put them into the lowest hell... [Good angels] will throw them on that day into the oven of burning fire, that the Lord of the spirits may avenge himself on them on account of their injustice, because they became subject to Satan, and have led astray those who dwell on earth."

And,

> And I saw there the hosts of the angels of punishment walking and holding chains of iron and metal.

Hell is a place of never-ending torment (21:7-10; 98:3).

> And from there I went to another place which was still more terrible than the former. And I saw a terrible thing: a great fire was there, which burned and flickered...; it was bounded by a complete abyss, great columns of fire were allowed to fall into it..." And at that time I said: "How terrible

The Evolution of a Revolution

> this place is, and painful to look at!" At that time answered Uriel, one of the holy angels, who was with me: "Enoch... this is the prison of the angels, and here they are held in eternity."

And,

> [I]n shame and in murder and in great poverty their spirits will be cast into an oven of fire.

Eternal life will be granted to the just (71:13-17).

> And the Head of days came with Michael and Gabriel, Rafael and Fanuel, and with thousands and with ten thousand times ten thousand angels without number. And the angel came to me and said: "Thou art a son of man who was born to justice, and justice dwells over thee, and the justice of the Head of days will not depart from thee." [Peace to those, his chosen]...long life will be with the Son of man, and peace will be to the just, and his right path to the just, in the name of the Lord of the spirits to all eternity.

Those who have their names inscribed in the Book of Life (i.e., the chosen) will shine like the stars (58:2-3; 104:1-4).

> Blessed are ye, the just and chosen, for your portion is glorious. And the just will be in the light of the sun, and the chosen in the light of everlasting life.

And,

> I swear to you just ones, that in heaven the angels will have a remembrance concerning you for good before the glory of the Great One. Your names will be written before the glory of the Great One... ye will shine like the luminaries of heaven, and will be seen, and the portals of heaven will be opened to you... Hope, and do not cease your hope, for ye will

The Evolution of a Revolution

have great joy, like the angels in heaven.

New Heavens and a New Earth

There will be a new heaven and a new earth (45:3-6).

> On that day the Chosen One will sit upon the throne of glory... on that day I will cause my Chosen One to dwell among them, and will transform heaven and make it a blessing and a light eternally. And I will transform the earth and make it a blessing, and will cause my chosen ones to dwell thereon; and those who have committed sins and crimes will not step on it... for the sinners there awaits before me a judgement, that I may destroy them from the face of the earth.

The earth will rejoice in the regeneration that attends the Messianic era (51:4-5).

> And in those days the mountains will skip like rams, and the hills spring like lambs satisfied with milk, and they will all be angels in heaven. Their faces will shine in gladness, because the Chosen One has arisen in those days, and the earth will rejoice, and the just will live thereon, and the chosen will walk and move thereon.

Defeated nations will finally pay homage to the victorious Son of Man—the Messiah (48:1-10).

> And at that place [i.e., Paradise] I saw an inexhaustible fountain of justice... And at that hour that the Son of man was called near the Lord of the spirits, and his name before the Head of days... All who live upon the earth will fall down before him and bend the knee to him, and will bless and praise him and sing songs to the name of the Lord of the spirits. For this purpose he was chosen and hidden

The Evolution of a Revolution

> before him before the world was created, and he will be before him to eternity... for in his name they will be saved... And on the day of their trouble, there will be rest on the earth; before him they will fall and not rise again, and there will be no one to take them with his hands and lift them up, because they have denied the Lord of the spirits and his Anointed.

Throngs will gather around the enthroned Lord, and forever sing His praises (14:16-23; 39:10-13).

> [I]ts floor was fire... and its ceiling was also a flaming fire. And I looked therein and saw a high throne; its appearance was like the hoar-frost, and its circuit like a shining sun and voices of the Cherubim. And from under the great throne came streams of flaming fire, and it was impossible to look at it... None of the angels were able to enter, nor any flesh to look upon the form of the face of the Majestic and Honored One. Fire of flaming fire was round him, and a great fire stood before him, and none of those who were around him could approach him; ten thousand times ten thousand were before him... And the holy ones who were near him did not leave day or night....

And,

> Before him there is no ceasing... Thee they praise who do not sleep; they stand before thy glory, and bless and glorify and exalt thee, saying: "Holy! Holy! Holy! the Lord of the spirits fills the earth with spirits." And here my eyes saw all those who do not sleep, standing before him, and they say: "Blessed art thou, and blessed the name of the Lord to all eternity."

There will be good reason to offer up continual, jubilant

The Evolution of a Revolution

praise; for planted in Paradise is a tree with a fragrance that causes sorrow and sickness to cease (25:3-7). In short, members of the regenerated commonwealth will enjoy a cessation of all evils—*at last there will be genuine peace and happiness!*

> [Michael the archangel answers Enoch's inquiry about the special tree in paradise]... And this tree of beautiful fragrance cannot be touched by any flesh until the time of the great judgment; when all things will be atoned for and consummated for eternity, this will be given to the just and the humble. And its fruits will be given to the chosen; it will be planted towards the north, in a holy place, toward the house of the Lord, the Eternal King. Then they will rejoice greatly, and be glad in the Holy One; they will let its fragrance enter their members, and live a long life upon the earth, as thy fathers lived; and in their days no sorrow or sickness or trouble or affliction will touch them." Then I blessed the Lord of glory, the Eternal King, because he had prepared such for the just men, and had created such....

Summary of 1 Enoch

I observe that 1 Enoch contains an eschatological picture akin to the New Testament's picture. There's a Tribulation Period during which time wickedness/lawlessness increases; there's a changing of the times and seasons, etc. Additionally, as is likewise the case with the New Testament, in Enoch we learn of the advent of a Messiah who will come and make war with the wicked in a climactic battle that results in the termination of the period of tribulation and the arrival of the Messianic era of peace and tranquility. Following this, Enoch informs that there will be a judgment, at which time God, called the "Ancient of Days," will give to everyone their

The Evolution of a Revolution

recompense: the wicked will be cast into the netherworld, to spend eternity engulfed in a lake of fire; the "chosen" and "just" will enjoy eternal bliss on a new heaven and a new earth.

Having observed all of this—and more—in 1 Enoch, we'll now consider how other Jewish documents likewise employed this imagery. Specifically, we will now go on to consider 4 Ezra.

Fourth Book of Ezra
Introduction

Although it's known in the English apocrypha as 2 Esdras, the text in view will be referred to as 4 Ezra, from its Latin name *Esdrae liber IV*. The Latin and Oriental versions seem to rely on an underlying Greek text; however, there's good reason to believe that the original Greek text was a translation of a Semitic original—Aramaic or Hebrew.[128]

4 Ezra really comes in two parts: chapters 1-2 and 15-16 (the beginning and end) are likely interpolations added by a Christian redactor[129]; chapters 3-14 consist of assorted dialogues and visions regarding the fate of Israel, sin, suffering, death, judgment of the wicked, the "heavenly Zion," the Messiah, the end of the age, etc.[130]

The scholarly consensus is that this Jewish text was composed around 100AD, thus making it contemporaneous with parts of the New Testament. Dr. Bruce Metzger, professor of New Testament language and literature at Princeton University, opines that similarities between 4 Ezra and the New Testament abound.[131] As was the case in 1 Enoch, here too we

---

[128] See Bruce Metzger, "The Fourth Book of Ezra," *The Old Testament Pseudepigrapha*, Vol. I., pp. 519-520.

[129] See Dr. W. Sanday's preface in G. H. Box's *The Ezra Apocalypse* (London: Sir Isaac Pitman & Sons, 1912), p. 5; and Bruce Metzger, "The Fourth Book of Ezra" *The Old Testament Pseudepigrapha*, Vol. I., p. 517.

[130] Bruce Metzger, "The Fourth Book of Ezra," *The Old Testament Pseudepigrapha*, Vol. I., pp. 517-518.

[131] Dr. Metzger lists the following examples: 4 Ezra 7:7 and Matt. 7:13 (i.e., the narrow gate to paradise); 4 Ezra 8:3 and Matt. 22:14f; Lk. 13:23f (i.e., the saying, many were created but few will be saved); 4 Ezra 4:33 and Matt. 24:3; Lk. 21:7 (i.e., the question, how long will it be till the end?); 4 Ezra 7: [61] and Jms. 4:14

The Evolution of a Revolution

will find similarities between the vocabularies in 4 Ezra and the New Testament. Let's turn to the particulars and see how this is the case. As was the case with his treatment of 1 Enoch, here again this writer will first provide his readers with his reconstruction of the book's eschatology, after which he will then attend to the texts firsthand.

Reconstruction of the Eschatology in 4 Ezra
Arrangement of Material

4 Ezra takes up soteriological questions related to humanity's vitiation and redeemed mankind's eventual entrance into an eternal reward. Sin is understood to have entered the stage of the human drama through the "First Adam" (4 Ezra 3:21-22). Like the first man, all have sinned (4 Ezra 8:35), and as a result of this perfidy, few will inherit the world to come (4 Ezra 8:1-3). It's not God's will that any would perish (4 Ezra 8:59), and so salvation is made available. Entrance into the eternal bliss is awarded to those who walk the narrow way (4 Ezra 7:6-16).

In addition, 4 Ezra reflects an eschatological scenario very much akin to that of 4Q 286, the famous "Son of God Scroll" in the Dead Sea Scroll collection. Mindful of a termination of the present era, 4 Ezra tells of the particulars of the "end of the age" (4 Ezra 6:7[132]). Jews are informed that a period of unprecedented tribulation is predicted (4 Ezra 4:51-5:3). Salvation is promised to those who endure the tribulation (4 Ezra 6:25). The Messiah will come after the tribulation, in accordance with the signs; and His Kingdom will be manifest (4 Ezra 7:26-28). There are a host of end-time expressions employed, like: "number being fulfilled," "times and seasons," and "appointed" times (4

(i.e., the statement that people are like a mist... smoke); 4 Ezra 12:42 and 2 Pet. 2:19 (i.e., the view that prophecy is akin to a lamp shining in a dark place); 4 Ezra 13:10f and 2 Thess. 2:8 (picturing the Messiah's destruction of the wicked); and lastly 4 Ezra 13:32-39 and Rev. 7:9 and 14:1 (i.e., images of assorted Messianic woes).

[132] Additionally, vs. 20 refers to "the age which is about to pass away."

The Evolution of a Revolution

Ezra 4:36-37). There will then be a resurrection (4 Ezra 7:32), followed by a judgment day (4 Ezra 7:33). The righteous will shine like the sun (4 Ezra 7:97).

The above mentioned tribulation-deliverance scenario is reiterated and expanded upon in 4 Ezra: Ezra goes on to tell of specific signs in advance of the Messianic era (4 Ezra 9:1-6); he speaks of the appearance of a terrible kingdom in the last days (4 Ezra 12:13); and he informs that the Messiah will eventually destroy the nefarious hordes, thus displacing the evil kingdom and inaugurating a period of eternal bliss.

A Closer Look at 4 Ezra
Soteriology: Humanity's Vitiation and Personal Salvation
Sin entered the stage of the human drama through the *"First Adam"* (4 Ezra 3:21-22).

> ...the first Adam, clothing himself with the evil heart, transgressed and was overcome; and likewise all who were born of him. Thus the infirmity became inveterate....

All mankind is defiled; *all have sinned* (4 Ezra 8:35).

> For in truth, There is none of the earth-born who has not dealt wickedly, and those that exist who has not sinned.

As a result of this perfidy, *few will inherit the world to come* (4 Ezra 8:1-3).

> This age the Most High has made for many, but the age to come for few... Many have been created, but few shall be saved!

It's not God's will that any would perish (4 Ezra 8:59).

The Evolution of a Revolution

For the Most High willed not that men should come to destruction.

Salvation is available. Entrance into the eternal bliss is awarded to those who walk the *narrow way* (4 Ezra 7:6-16).

> There is a builded city which lies on level ground, and it is full of good things; but its entrance is narrow and lies on a steep, having fire on the right hand and deep water on the left; and there is only one path lying between them both, that is between the fire and the water (and so small) is this path, that it can only contain one man's footstep at once. If, now, this city be given to a man for an inheritance, unless the heir pass through the danger set before him, how shall he receive his inheritance? And I said: It is so Lord! Then said he unto me: Even so, also, is Israel's portion; for it was for their sakes that I made the world; but when Adam transgressed my statues, then that which had been made was judged: and then the "ways" of this world became narrow and sorrowful and painful and full of perils coupled with great toils. But the ways of the future world are broad and safe , and yield the fruit of immortality. If, then, the living shall not have surely entered into these narrow and vain things, they will not be able to receive what has been reserved for them.

Eschatology: Tribulation Period and the Messianic Era

There are a host of *end-time expressions* employed in this Jewish apocalyptic literature: e.g., "number being fulfilled," "times and seasons," and "appointed" times (4 Ezra 4:36-37).

> And to them the archangel Jeremiel made reply, and said: Even when the number of those like yourself is fulfilled! For he has weighed the age in the balance, And with measure has measured the times, and by number has numbered the seasons:

The Evolution of a Revolution

> Neither will he move nor stir things, till the measure appointed be fulfilled.

Mindful of a termination of the present era, people ask for the particulars of the *"end of the age"* (4 Ezra 6:7).

> Then I answered and said: What shall mark the parting asunder of the times? When shall the End of the first (age) and beginning of the second be?

Jews are informed that a period of unprecedented *tribulation* is predicted (4 Ezra 4:51-5:3).

> Then I made supplication and said: Thinkest thou that I shall live until those days? Who shall be in those days? He answered me, and said: As for the signs concerning which thou askest me... Behold the days come when the inhabitants of the earth shall be seized with great panic, and the way of truth will be hidden, and the land of faith be barren. And iniquity will be increased above that which thou seest or that thou hast heard of long ago. And the land that thou seest shall be a pathless waste; and men shall see it forsaken....

Salvation is promised to those who *endure* the tribulation (4 Ezra 6:25).

> And it shall be that whosoever shall have survived all these things that I have foretold unto thee, he shall be saved and shall see my salvation and the end of my world.

The *Messiah will come after the tribulation*, in accordance with the signs; His Kingdom will be manifest (4 Ezra 7:26-28).

For behold the days come, and shall be that when

The Evolution of a Revolution

the signs which I have foretold unto thee shall come to pass, then shall the city that now is invisible appear, and the land which is now concealed seen. And whoever is delivered from the predicted evils, the same shall see my wonders. For my *Son the Messiah* shall be revealed, together with those who are with him.... (Italics mine)

There will then be a *resurrection* (4 Ezra 7:32).

And the earth shall restore those that sleep in her, and the dust those that rest therein. And the chambers shall restore the souls that were commited unto them.

There will then be a *judgment* (4 Ezra 7:33).

And the Most High shall be revealed upon the throne of judgment: (and then cometh the end) and compassion shall pass away (and pity be far off) and long-suffering withdrawn, But judgment alone shall remain, truth shall stand, and faithfulness triumph. And recompense shall follow, and the reward be manifest; deeds of righteousness shall awake, and deeds of iniquity shall not sleep. And then shall the pit of torment appear and over against it the place of refreshment. The furnace of Gehenna shall be manifest and over against it the Paradise of delight. And then shall the Most High say to the nations that have been raised (from the dead): Look now and consider who you have denied, whom you have not served, whose commandments ye have despised. Look now before (you) here delight and refreshment, there fire and torments! Thus shall he speak unto them in the Day of Judgement. For thus shall the Day of Judgment be. (A day) whereon there is neither sun, nor moon, nor stars, neither clouds, nor thunder, nor lightning, Neither wind, nor rain-storm, nor cloud-rack, neither darkness, nor evening, nor morning; neither

The Evolution of a Revolution

> summer, nor autumn, nor winter; neither heat, nor frost, nor cold, neither hail, nor rain, nor dew, neither noon, nor night, nor dawn, neither shining, nor brightness, nor light save only the splendour of the brightness of the Most High, whereby all shall be destined to see what has been determined (for them).

The *righteous will shine like the sun* (4 Ezra 7:97).

> [T]heir face is destined to shine as the sun... [for] they are destined to be made like the light of the stars, henceforth incorruptable.

The tribulation-deliverance scenario is reiterated and expanded upon in 4 Ezra. :

A. Specific signs are enumerated that will precede the Messianic era (4 Ezra 9:1-6).

> Measure the matter carefully in thy mind, and when thou seest that a certain part of the predicted signs are past, then shalt thou understand that it is the very time when the Most High is about to visit the works which he has made. When in the world there shall appear quaking of places, tumult of peoples, scheming of nations, confusion of leaders, disquietude of princes, then shalt thou understand that it is of these things the Most High has spoke since the days that were aforetime from the beginning. For just as with respect to all that has happened in the world the beginning is obscure, but the end (issue) manifest, so also are the times of the Most High: the beginnings are [visible] in portents and secret signs, and then end in effects and marvels.

B. A terrible kingdom makes its appearance in the last days

The Evolution of a Revolution

(4 Ezra 12:13).

> Behold the days come when there shall arise a kingdom upon the earth, and it shall be more terrible than all the kingdoms that were before it.

C. The victorious Messiah displaces the evil kingdom.

> And after this I beheld, and Lo! all who were gathered together against him to wage war with him were seized with great fear; yet they dared to fight. And lo! when he saw the assault of the multitude as they came he neither lifted his hand nor held spear nor any war-like weapon; but I saw only how he sent out of his mouth as it were a fiery stream, and out of his lips a flaming breath, and out of his tongue he shot forth a storm of sparks. And these were all mingled together—the firey stream, the flaming breath, and.. the storm; and they fell upon the assault of the multitude which was prepared to fight, and burned them all up, so that suddenly nothing more was to be seen of the innumerable multitude save only the dust of the ashes and the smell of smoke. When I saw this I was amazed.

D. Summary: Messiah/God's Son delivers the godly.

> Behold the days come when the Most High is about to deliver them that are upon the earth. And there shall come astonishment of mind upon the dwellers on earth: and they shall plan to war one against the other, city against city, place against place, people against people, and kingdom against kingdom. And it shall be when these things shall come to pass, and the signs shall happen which I shewed thee before, then shall my Son be revealed whom thou didst see as a man ascending... But he shall stand upon the summit of Mount Sion. [And Sion

The Evolution of a Revolution

shall come and shall be manifest to all men, prepared and builded, even as thou didst see the mountain cut out without hands.] But he, my Son, shall reprove the nations that are come for their ungodliness... and then shall he destroy them without labor by the law which is compared to a fire.

Summary

A cursory examination of the material in Ezra discloses that there are indeed relationships between Jewish soteriology and eschatology and that reflected in the New Testament. Lastly, in what follows, we'll consider the Apocalypse of Baruch's testimony, wherein we'll also note the relationship between ancient "Jewish" and "Christian" understandings.

The Apocalypse of Baruch
Introduction

Dr. A. F. J. Klijn, writing an introduction about this Apocalpse in *Old Testament Pseudepigrapha,* alleges that there are three reasons why the work in question originated in Israel: (1) there was a Hebrew original of the work; (2) close relationships existed between Baruch and rabbinic literature; and (3) the author of the work—certainly not Baruch—took his stand with Jews residing in Judea and encouraged Jews in the diaspora.[133] Though the destruction of Jerusalem was given as the occasion for the writing, it is generally understood that the text was written after 70AD, making it a contemporary of some of the New Testament books.

The writer was interested in the Temple; this, according to Klijin, served as a suitable starting point for his questioning Israel's fate now that it was without the sacred Sanctuary. Israel's destiny is of paramount importance to the author. In what follows, I will focus on Baruch's eschatological vision in

---

[133] *The Old Testament Pseudepigrapha,* Vol. I, p. 617.

The Evolution of a Revolution

general, and his vision of Messianic redemption in particular.[134]

Reconstructing Baruch's Eschatology
Arrangement of Material

To summarize Baruch, the earth's inhabitants will be seized with terror, pressed from all sides during the Tribulation (Bar. 25:1-4), a period that comes replete with: commotions, death, desolation, famine, earthquakes, terrors, portents, oppression and wickedness (Bar. 27:1-15). During this period there will be a multiplication of wars, rumors of wars and assorted cataclysmic events (Bar. 48:31-39). Hatred will greatly increase, wars and murders will be common place, treachery will become normative, and people will devour one another (Bar. 70:2-10). Wickedness will escalate through a succession of evil kingdoms, the last of which will be more nefarious than the previous ones: it will be the kingdom of the wicked ruler of the period of Great Tribulation. Finally, the Messiah will come, destroy the wicked and bring the period to a close (Bar. 39:3-7).

The Messiah's arrival will bring an end to the earthly hostilities. Upon His advent, the world will experience rejuvenation (Bar. 29:3-8). A resurrection of the dead will also accompany His coming. This assemblage of the deceased will occur at what Baruch calls "the consummation of the times" (Bar. 30:1-3). There will be a judgment with adjudication based on how folk treated the "Seed of Jacob" (Bar. 72:2-4). The

---

[134] Klijn went on to outline the book as follows: 1:1-8:8, Destruction of Jerusalem by the Babylonians; 9:1-12:4, Baruch's Lamentation Following his Fast; 12:5-20:4, Questions about Righteousness and Avoiding Corruption; 20:5-30:5, Baruch's Predictions: Disasters are Coming, the Messiah's Coming follows, as does the Resurrection of the Dead and a Final Judgment; 31:1-34:1, Warning of Disaster in the End of Days; 35:1-43:3, Vision of the Forest; 44:1-46:7, Baruch Speaks on God's Judgment; 47:1-48:50, Baruch's Understanding of God's Predetermination; 49:1-52:7, The Outward Appearance of the Righteous after the Resurrection; 53:1-74:4, The Vision of the Cloud with Bright and Dark Waters; 75:1-77:26, The Saving of the Righteous; 78:1-87:1, An Exhortation to Faithfulness to the Jewish Tribes in the Dispersion (*Ibid.*, p. 615).

The Evolution of a Revolution

perfidious leader of the tribulation kingdom will also be judged (Bar. 40:1-3). Some will be saved—"by their works," according to the apocalypse—and they will be delivered from the Tribulation, shine like the stars, and inherit Paradise (Bar. 51:7-14).

With the judgment of the world complete, the Messiah will bring about a period of peace and prosperity—the Messianic era. Sin, death and disease will vanish; man and animal will exist peacefully, side by side. In short, the creation will return to the state that existed in the Garden of Eden—Paradise restored (Bar. 73:1-7).

A Closer Look at the Apocalypse of Baruch
Dire Tribulation

The earth's inhabitants will be panic stricken, pressed from all sides by a dire Tribulation period that ends with the Messiah's arrival (25:1-4).

> Thou too shalt be kept safely till that time till that sign which the Most High will work for the inhabitants of the earth in the end of days. This therefore will be the sign. When a stupor shall seize the inhabitants of the earth, and they shall fall into many tribulations, and again when they fall into great torments. And it shall come to pass when they say in their thoughts by reason of their much tribulation: 'The Mighty One doth no longer remember the earth'—yea, it will come to pass when they abandon hope, that the time will then awake.

The tribulation period comes replete with: commotions, death, desolation, famine, earthquakes, terrors, portents, oppression and wickedness (27:1-15).

> And He answered and said unto me: "Into twelve parts is that time [i.e., the tribulation period]

The Evolution of a Revolution

divided... In the first part there will be the beginnings of commotions. And in the second part (there will be) slayings of great ones. And in the third part (there will be) the fall of many by death. And in the fourth part the sending of desolation. And in the fifth part famine and withholding of rain. And in the sixth part earthquakes and terrors... multitude of portents and incursions... fall of fire... rapine and much oppression... wickedness and unchastity... Confusion and the mingling together of those things aforesaid... [this period is called, then] the consummation of the times."

There will come a succession of evil kingdoms, the last of which will be more nefarious than the first—it will be that of the ruler of the tribulation period. Finally, the Messiah will come, destroy the wicked and close the period (39:3-7).

Behold! the days come, and this kingdom will be destroyed which once destroyed Zion, and it will be subjected to that which comes after it. Moreover, that also again after a time will be destroyed, and another, a third, will arise, and that also will have dominion for its time, and will be destroyed. And after these things a fourth kingdom will arise, whose power will be harsh and evil far beyond those which were before it... And by it the truth will be hidden, and those who are polluted with iniquity will flee to it... And it will come to pass when the time of his consummation when he should fall has approached, then the principate of My Messiah will be revealed, which is like the fountain and the vine, and when it is revealed it will root out the multitude of his host.

During the tribulation there will be a multiplication of wars, rumors of wars and assorted cataclysmic events (48:31-39).

For that time will arise which brings affliction; for

The Evolution of a Revolution

> it will come and pass by with quick vehemence, and it will be turbulent coming in the heat of indignation. And it will come to pass in those days that all the inhabitants of the earth will be moved one against another... For there will not be found many wise at that time, and the intelligent will be but a few... And there will be rumors and tidings not a few, and the works of portents will be shown... many will be roused in anger to injure many, and they will rouse up armies in order to shed blood, and in the end they will perish together with them. And it will come to pass at the self-same time, that a change of times will manifestly appear to every man... Therefore a fire will consume their thoughts... for the Judge will come and will not tarry.

Some will be saved—"by their works," according to the apocalypse—and they will be delivered from the tribulation, shine like the stars, and inherit Paradise (51:7-14).

> But those who have been saved by their works... they will behold the world which is now invisible to them, and they will behold the time which is now invisible to them... they shall be made like the angels, and be made equal to the stars, and they shall be changed into every form they desire, from beauty into loveliness, and from light into the splendor of glory. For there will be spread before them the extents of Paradise, and there will be shown to them the beauty of the majesty of the living creatures which are beneath the throne, and all the armies of the angels, who are held fast by a command, that they may stand in their places till their advent comes. Moreover there will then be excellency in the righteous surpassing that in the angels. For the first will receive the last, those whom they were expecting, and the last those of whom they used to hear that they had passed

The Evolution of a Revolution

away. For they have been delivered from this world of tribulation, and laid down the burden of anguish.

During the tribulation period hatred will greatly increase, wars and murders will be common place, as treachery becomes normative: people will devour one another (70:2-10).

> Behold! the days come, and it will be when the time of the age has ripened, and the harvest of its evil and good seeds has come, that the Mighty One will bring upon the earth and its inhabitants and upon its rulers perturbation of spirit and stupor of heart. And they will hate one another, and provoke one another to fight, and the mean will rule over the honourable... it will come when those things which were predicted have come to pass, that confusion will fall upon all men, and some of them will fall in battle, and some of them will perish in anguish, and some of them will be destroyed by their own. Then the Most High will reveal to those peoples whom He has prepared, and they will come and make war with the leaders that shall then be left. And it shall come to pass that whosoever gets safe out of the war will die in the earthquake, and whosoever gets safe out of the earthquake will be burned by the fire, and whosoever gets safe out of the fire will be destroyed by famine. [And it will come to pass that whosoever of the victors and the vanquished gets safe out of and escapes all these things aforesaid will be delivered into the hands of My servant Messiah.] For all the earth will devour its inhabitants.

Finally, the Messiah will come and judge the nations of the earth on the basis of how they treated God's Old Testament covenant people—i.e., the "Chosen People" (72:2-4).

After the signs have come, of which thou wast told

The Evolution of a Revolution

before, when the nations become turbulent, and the time of My Messiah is come, He will both summon all the nations, and some of them He will spare, and some of them He will slay... Every nation which knows not Israel, and has not trodden down the seed of Jacob, shall indeed be spared.

The Arrival of the Victorious Messiah

The Messiah comes, ending the period of hostility. Upon His arrival, the world experiences rejuvenation (29:3-8).

> And it will come to pass when all is accomplished that... the Messiah will then begin to be revealed. And Behemoth will be revealed from his place, and Leviathan will ascend from the sea, those two great sea monsters which I created in the fifth day of creation, and I kept them until that time... The earth will also yield its fruit ten thousand fold, and on one vine there will be a thousand branches, and each branch will produce a thousand clusters, and each cluster will produce a thousand grapes, and each grape will produce a core of wine. And those who have hungered will rejoice: moreover, also, they will behold marvels every day... the treasury of manna will again descend from on high, and they will eat of it in those years, because these are they who have come to the consummation of time.

A resurrection of the dead will accompany the Messiah's arrival. This assemblage of the deceased will occur at what Baruch calls "the consummation of the times"—what we refer to as the "end of days" (30:1-3).

> And it will come to pass after these things, when the time of the advent of the Messiah is fulfilled, and He will return in glory, then all who have fallen asleep in hope of Him shall rise again. And

The Evolution of a Revolution

> it will come to pass at that time that the treasuries will be opened in which is preserved the number of the souls of the righteous, and they will come forth, and a multitude of souls will be seen together in one assemblage of one thought, and the first will rejoice and the last will be grieved. For he knows that the time has come of which it is said, that it is the consummation of the times....

The perfidious Tribulation-period leader is judged (40:1-3).

> The leader of that time will be left alive, when the multitude of his hosts will be put to the sword and be bound, and they will take him up to Mount Zion, and My Messiah will convict him of all his impieties, and will gather and set before him all the works of his hosts. And afterwards he will put him to death... And his [i.e., God's] principate will stand forever, until the world of corruption is at end, and until the times aforesaid are fulfilled.

With the judgment on the world complete, the Messiah then brings about a period of peace and prosperity—the long-awaited Messianic era. Sin, death and disease will vanish, and man and nature will be restored to have communion with God and one another. In short, the creation returns to the state that existed in the Garden of Eden—Paradise restored (73:1-7).

> And it will come to pass, when He has brought low everything that is in the world, and has sat down in peace for the age on the throne of His kingdom, that joy will then be revealed and rest appear. And then healing will descend in dew, and disease will withdraw, and anxiety and anguish and lamentation will pass from amongst men, and gladness will proceed through the whole earth. And no one shall again die untimely, nor shall any adversity

The Evolution of a Revolution

suddenly befall... And wild beasts will come from the forest and minister unto men, and asps and dragons will come forth from their holes to submit themselves to a little child. And women will no longer have pain when they bear, nor will they suffer torment when they yield the fruit of the womb.

Summary
Old Testament Influences on Jewish and Christian Eschatological Language

Is there a relationship between ancient Jewish and Christian literature? Professor Donald Hagner, of the Fuller Theological Seminary, says that "The rabbis and Jesus share[d] the expectation of a coming eschatological kingdom of God to be realized on earth. The nature of the kingdom would have been agreed on essentially, if not altogether, by the rabbis and Jesus."[135] From the selected samplings in this chapter, that Dr. Hagner is correct should be obvious. If it isn't, read on.

The above may be a "tough pill for some to swallow." I believe that in order to be intellectually honest, we must admit that *there are, in fact, similarities between the ancient Jewish and the "inspired" Christian writings.* Refusing to look at the evidence, and/or pretending that similarities don't exist, is not an option for evangelical scholars. Once we decide to face the fact head-on—hopefully without being angry at those who bring the information to our attention—we can then do the following: resolve the seeming crisis, deepen our understanding of the New Testament and the New Testament's world, and grow as persons through the experience.

We shouldn't be surprised that similarities exist. Both ancient Christians and ancient Jews shared the same Old Testament. In that it contains eschatological reflections of a period of tribulation, a coming Messiah, a messianic era, and a

---

[135] Donald Hagner, *The Jewish Reclaimation of Jesus* (Grand Rapids: Academie Books, 1984), p. 140.

The Evolution of a Revolution

final judgment one could reasonably expect that Jewish Bible teachers would pick up on these themes.

The idealized age of global peace and spiritual regeneration, articulated in the Old Testament was never realized during the Old Testament period. The Jewish Bible closes with a host of unappeased longings and unfulfilled prophecies. The prophets envisioned a time, in the future, when the Glory of the Lord would shine forth upon (and from) a regenerated people, resting securely in their Promised Land—i.e., Israel (cf., e.g. Hosea 3:4-5; Jere. 23:5-6; Ezek. 37:24-28; Zech. 8:7-8). Israel's "faithful" awaited (and await, for that matter) the renewal of the once splendid, though short lived, Davidic Empire—to be ruled by the Messiah Himself. The prophets knew that in advance of the promised Messianic era the earth's inhabitants would undergo a series of global upheavals, major wars, etc. (cf., e.g. Zech. 12:1-14:21; Dan. 11:1-45), but that peace would eventually come when the Prince of Peace arrived. He, the Messiah, would bring about a cessation of global hostilities (cf., e.g. Isa. 2:4); additionally, He would inaugurate a period of global regeneration (cf., e.g. Amos 9:13-14; Ezek. 34:26-29) and even a resurrection of the dead (Dan. 12: 2). In sum, under His administration it was envisioned that the earth would experience a period of total health and healing (Isa. 33:24; 35:5-6) resulting, of course, in great joy and peace (Isa. 51:11).

The eschatological language of Jewish pseudepigrapha is greatly flavored by the Old Testament, as is the New Testament. *The fact that both rely heavily on the Old Testament accounts for their similarities.*

From the above, we see that Jesus' proclamation of a coming Messianic Kingdom was quintessentially a Jewish announcement. His preaching was, among other things, based to a large extent on the Old Testament. *Jesus' kerygmatic message of the Kingdom of God was also articulated using the prevailing*

The Evolution of a Revolution

Judaic nomenclature, expository techniques and imagery. For these and many other reasons, I see Jesus' message as fitting well within the boundaries of first century Jewish apocalyptic language—something that will be abudantly clear, I believe, after reading the following.

C. Meeting at the Crossroads: Jesus' "Lord's Prayer" and Judaism's "Kaddish"
Introduction

With the sound of ancient Jewish eschatology ringing in our ears, this is perhaps a good time to begin introducing the New Testament more directly into the conversation. In what follows, I'll demonstrate how Jesus' prayer, called the "Lord's Prayer," grows out of the OT's eschatological expectations as reflected in ancient Jewish pseudepigrapha. I'll do this, as the old Beatles' song goes "with a little help from my friends."

Brad Young, a Christian, completed a B.A. (major in Greek with a minor in Hebrew) at Oral Roberts University and then went to Israel where he studied under Professor David Flusser—Israel's leading Jewish NT scholar[136]—and took an M.A. and Ph.D. in early Christianity and early Judaism at Hebrew University.[137] With his exposure to the primary sources from *both* ancient Jewish and Christian worlds, Professor Young is able to provide wonderful insights on what's commonly called the "Lord's Prayer"—a misnomer.

I have provided my own juxtaposition of Dr. Young's Hebrew reconstruction of the NT's "Lord's Prayer," along with the present Greek and likely Hebrew original.[138] I would encourage you to take special note of Dr. Young's English translation, and compare it with your version. (See footnote for the KJV.)

---

[136] Relevant here would be Flusser's book *Jewish Sources in Early Christianity*, trans. John Glucker (Tel Aviv: MOD, 1989).

[137] Young's doctoral dissertation was published under the title *Jesus and His Jewish Parables* (New York: Paulist Press, 1989).

[138] Brad Young, *The Jewish Background to the Lord's Prayer* (Dayton, OH: Center for Judaic Christian Studies, 1984).

The Evolution of a Revolution

After reflecting on Dr. Young's rendition for a moment, I'd ask my readers to consider Judaism's "Kaddish," which I've made available, in full. The קדש (*Kaddish* = "holy") was originally an Aramaic doxology used by ancient Jews—Jesus included. In the "Kaddish," you will note how God's name is extolled. The expression "May his great name be blessed for all eternity" is an Ashkenazic Jewish version, that in Sephardic Jewish circles reads: "May he make his salvation closer and bring his Messiah near."[139] In what follows, we'll see how the Messiah(i.e., Jesus Christ) used this Jewish petition—pay close attention to the following.

Young's Version of "The Lord's Prayer":

> Our Father who is in heaven, may your name be sanctified. May you continue establishing your kingdom; May your will be done in heaven and on earth. Give us this day our daily portion. Forgive us our sins as we also have forgiven those who have sinned against us. Do not bring us into the grasp of temptation, but deliver us from the evil one.[140]

Greek and Hebrew Texts

Greek:	Hebrew Reconstruction:
(6:9) Πάτερ ἡμῶν ὁ ἐν τοῖς οὐρανοῖς, ἁγιασθήτω τὸ ὄνομά σου·	אבינו שבשמים יתקדש שמך
(6:10) ἐλθέτω ἡ βασιλεία σου, ὡς ἐν οὐρανῷ καὶ ἐπὶ γῆς·	מליך מלכותך יעשה רצונך בשמים ובארץ
(6:11) τὸν ἄρτον ἡμῶν τὸν ἐπιούσιον δὸς ἡμῖν σήμερον·	את לחם חוקנו תן לנו היום
(6:12) καὶ ἄφες ἡμῖν τὰ ὀφειλήματα ἡμῶν, ὡς καὶ ἡμεῖς ἀφήκαμεν τοῖς	ומחול לנו את חובותינו כאשר מחלנו גם אנחנו לחייבינו

---

[139] *Encyclopaedia Judaica*, Vol 10, pp. 660-662.

[140] Compare this with the KJV: 9 "Our Father which art in heaven, Hallowed be thy name. 10 Thy kingdom come. Thy will be done in earth, as it is in heaven. 11 Give us this day our daily bread. 12 And forgive us our debts, as we forgive our debtors. 13 And lead us not into temptation, but deliver us from evil: For thine is the kingdom, and the power, and the glory, for ever. Amen."

The Evolution of a Revolution

ὀφειλέταις ἡμῶν·
(6:13) καὶ μὴ εἰσενέγκῃς ἡμᾶς εἰς πειρασμόν, ἀλλὰ ῥῦσαι ἡμᾶς ἀπὸ τοῦ πονηροῦ.

ואל תביאנו לידי נסיון אלא תצילנו מן הרע

The Kaddish—Verse by Verse

Let his name be glorifed and sanctified throughout the universe which he created according to his purpose. May he bring about the reign of his kingdom in your lifetime, in your days, and in the lifetime of all the house of Israel, speedily, soon! And let all say, "Amen.

יתגדל ויתקדש שמט רבא בעלמא די ברא כרעותה וימליך מלכותה בחייכון וביומיכון ובחיי דכל בית ישראל בעגלא ובזמן קריב ואמרו אמן

And then, after a congregational response, the following is recited:

Blessed and praised, glorified and exalted, extolled and honored, magnified and lauded, be the name of the Holy One, blessed be he, although he is far greater than all blessing, hymns, praises, and songs which are offered in the world; and all say, "amen."

יתברך וישתבח ותיפאר ותרומם ויתנשא ויתהדר ויתעלה ויתהלל שמה דקדשא בריך הוא אעלא לעלא מן כל ברכתא תשירתא תשבחתא ונחמתא דאמירן בעלמא ואמרואמן

And then:

May there be great peace from heaven and life for us and all Israel; and say, "amen."

יהא שלמא רבא מן שמיא וחיים עלינו ועל כל ישראל ואמרו אמן

The Evolution of a Revolution

Followed lastly with:

> He who makes peace in the heavenly realms, may he make peace for us and for all Israel; and say, "amen."

עשה שלום במרומיו הוא יעשה שלום עלינו ועל כל ישראל ואמרו אמן

Evaluation

A cursory examination, alone, should suffice to demonstrate the point: there is a relationship between the *Jewish* "Kaddish" and the *Christian* "Lord's Prayer." In what follows—leaning on Professor Young, for the most part—we'll consider a few aspects of the genetic linkage.

Dr. Young, in his *The Jewish Background to the Lord's Prayer*, observed the frequent usage of the expression ברוך השם ("Bless the Name") and קדש השם ("Sanctify the Name [of the Lord]").[141] Worthy of note here, of course, is how interest in God's Name and His coming Kingdom is quite evident in the Jewish prayer above—much as in the pseudepigraphal literature. Dr. Young imparts that the Semitic idiom speaks of a kingdom that is unfolding; thus he translates: *"May you continue establishing your kingdom"* (תמליך מלכותך).[142] He sees—as do a number of Jewish thinkers—a process here and *not* an eschatological event. Dr. Young finds the typical translation of the Matthean expression "for theirs is the kingdom of heaven" wanting, preferring the Greek partitive genitive "the kingdom is comprised of such as these."[143]

---

[141] Furthermore, after pronouncing יהוה (i.e., the "Tetragrammaton") on Yom Kippur, the people of Israel said, much like Jesus here, that: "His [i.e., God's] honorable name is blessed and his Kingdom is forever and ever. (*Ibid.*, p. 14: culled, by Dr. Young, from Yoma 3:8, 6:2; Sotah 7:6; b. Yoma 35b; j Yoma, chap. 3 *halacha* 3, 40b; and parallels).

[142] *Ibid.*, pp. 11-12.

[143] *Ibid.*, p. 16.; see also n. 2 above.

The Evolution of a Revolution

In regard the accomplishment of God's will, the following from the intertestamental book of 1 Maccabees 3:60 may be helpful. Reconstructing from Greek to Hebrew, Dr. Young ascertained "Even as his will is in heaven, so let it be done."[144] Young sees a connection between this and the following short petition from an ancient Jewish sage, Rabbi Eleazar: "Do your will in heaven [O Lord] and grant satisfaction to those who fear you on earth..." (Tos. Ber. 3:7; b. Ber. 16b).[145] The point should be obvious: the *Jewish petitions, like Jesus' petition, ask for God's will to be accomplished on earth as in heaven.*

As for Jesus' statement that is usually translated "give us this day our daily bread," Dr. Young prefers "tomorrow's food" over "daily bread." Furthermore, he believes that St. Jerome had the Hebrew *Gospel of the Nazarenes* in view (see chapter I.) which read מחר (machar), "tomorrow"; and that "daily" (*epiousion*) exists nowhere else except here.[146] In Pro. 30:8 we find the expression לחם חקי—i.e., "food that is needful for me," speaking of the necessary amount to survive. To paraphrase then, the "Lord's Prayer" requests for God to attend to that which is *absolutely necessary to sustain life*—a far cry from the erroneous "Prosperity" doctrine made popular in some circles in recent days.

In his translation of Jesus saying "forgive us our trespasses as we forgive those who trespass against us," Young is again helpful, noting that in 170AD the Jewish sage Ben Sira said: "Forgive your neighbor the wrong he has done, and then your sins will be pardoned when you pray" (Ben Sira 28:2-4),[147] and "Everyone who is merciful to others will receive mercy from heaven." Additionally, other sages taught that everyone who does *not* show mercy to others will *not* receive mercy from

---

[144] *Ibid.*, p. 43, n. 23.
[145] *Ibid.*, p. 19.
[146] *Ibid.*, p. 22.
[147] As for those who have wronged us: "obligated" and "debtors" = "sinners," as well.

heaven" (Yoma 8:9). All this evidences a Jewish view very much *akin* to Jesus' petition, does it not?[148]

Finally, Jesus' saying "deliver us from evil" evidences many similarities with ancient Judaism.[149] From the *Dead Sea Scrolls*, in cave 11, we hear the sectary praying "Let not Satan nor an unclean spirit rule over me"(ורוח טמאה אל תשלט בי שטן). From the *Testament of Levi* we likewise hear: "And do not let Satan rule over me to lead me astray"; and, of course, from Ps. 119:133 we hear "...let no iniquity get dominion over me." Lastly, in the Talmud, b. Ber. 16b we read:

> May it be pleasing before You O Lord and God of our fathers, to deliver us from insolence and insolent men, from an evil man, from contact with evil, from the evil inclination, from an evil companion, from an evil neighbor, and from Satan who destroys....

This should suffice as ample proof of ancient Jewish views very much akin to Jesus' views. With Professor Young's help, we have examined the "Lord's Prayer" as it might have been understood by those who first heard and recited it—*Jews*.

D. Paul's Contextualization of Judaism's Eschatological Message
Introduction

Previously, we noted that Paul successfully contextualized the Gospel to service the needs and interests of his non-Jewish constituents in the Greco-Roman world, and that, in the process, he stirred up some of the original Jewish believers, who thought that his innovations were unacceptable, because they didn't conform to the Jewish norms that prevailed in their circles. Here I will argue that though innovative, *Paul's*

---
[148] *Ibid.*, p. 29.
[149] *Ibid.*, p. 32.

The Evolution of a Revolution

message to the Greeks, like Jesus' message to the Jews, was still quintessentially a Jewish message—and a good Jewish message at that! Here, I will hopefully prove the point through my examination of Paul's epistle to the Philippians—an epistle written to *non*-Jews.

Philippi was a small city founded by Alexander the Great's father, Phillip of Macedonia. In 42 B.C.E. a famous battle was fought nearby: Brutus's and Cassius's forces went up against Anthony's and Octavian's. Following the war, Philippi became a Roman colony and came to enjoy a privileged position in the empire. Luke records that Paul established a church there on his second missionary journey (Acts 16). We know that, unlike with Corinth, Paul seemed to enjoy a rather cordial relationship with this community. He was helped by them in various ways; this correspondence was for them a "thank you letter"—for us it may serve as a window into Paul's Jewish thought-world.

In this section, relying on the Philippian epistle, I will attempt to probe Paul's inner world to ascertain how he understood Jesus Christ to be the catalyst for Judaism's long-awaited Messainic age. Specifically, I will examine what Paul is saying about God in the Philippian correspondence, and then I will raise the question as to the likely source of those views—as you may have guessed, *I'll argue for a Jewish source.* I will give my readers access to lively theological conversation. ("lively"!? In truth, for some it may be quite boring.) Lastly, I will turn our attention to the governing metaphor of Philippians: the "Christ Hymn," so called. Here, I will compare an ancient Jewish hymn, the "Aleynu" (עלינו), to the Philippian locus explicated in this chapter's first two sections. At the close, I will demonstrate how that Paul—the Apostle to the Gentiles—was, nonetheless, first of all, a Jewish theologian bent on contextualizing Jesus' Jewish message for his non-Jewish constituents.

The Evolution of a Revolution

Paul's Views on God

What does Paul say about God in the Philippian letter? and, What influenced his perspective? The following may seem a bit pedestrian; yet, a basic introduction to Pauline Christology is in order. Here now is how Paul speaks of his *God* (יהוה/θεός), his *Lord* (ישוע/κύριος), his *Messiah/Christ* (משיח/Χριστός), and the *Holy Spirit* (רוח/πνεῦμα).

God/Jehovah
The Philippian Text

Jehovah is the God of *peace and grace* (1:2; 4:7);[150] He's *thanked* (1:3); He's a *witness* to Paul's earnestness on behalf of the Philippian community (1:8); He's to be *glorified and praised* through Jesus Christ (1:11; 4:20); there's a *Word of God* that's proclaimed (1:14); *salvation* is from God (1:28); *Jesus was in God's form* yet He divested Himself of His rank to serve humanity (2:6); *He exalts Jesus* following His humiliation (2:9); *God receives glory in and through Jesus' sacrifice* (2:11); *He's at work* in the Philippian community (2:13); He considers the Philippian congregants to be *His children* (2:15); He *heals sickness* (2:27); He desires *worship in Spirit* (3:3); He has/gives a *righteousness that comes through faith* (3:9); He has a *call*—i.e., women and men are summoned to Him (3:14); He *reveals His will* (3:15); *He wants us to petition Him instead of being anxious* (4:6, 19); and He is pleased because of the Church's sacrifice for Paul (4:18).

The Old Testament Subtext

It's worthy of note that Paul's God is the God of His fathers. He's *Jehovah-Jireh* (יהוה יראה, "God will Provide") in Gen. 22:13-14 (cf., 3:15; 4:6, 19); *Jehovah-Rapha* (יהוה רפאך, "God Healeth") in Ex. 15:26 (cf., 2:27). He's *Jehovah-Shalom* (יהוה שלום, "God our Peace") in Judges 6:24 (cf., 1: 2; 4:7); He's

---

[150] All enclosed reference numbers refer to the Philippian text.

The Evolution of a Revolution

Jehovah-Tsidkenu (צדקנו יהוה, "God our Righteousness") in Jere. 23:6 (cf., 3:9); and He's *Jehovah-Shammah* (שמה יהוה, "God is Present") in Ezek. 48:35. As far as God's various attributes go (e.g., righteousness, peacemaker, healer, etc.) they speak for themselves in the outline above.

Christ/Messiah

God is the father of the Lord Jesus Christ (1:2). The "Lord" of the Old Testament (אדני) is transformed into "Jesus" in the New Testament. Paul's God was a creator, e.g. "In the beginning God created the heavens and the earth" (cf. בראשית ברא אלהים,[151] Gen. 1:1). He's referred to as the Lord God (יהוה אלהים) who made the heavens and the earth in Gen. 2:4. What does Paul do with Judaism's creator God? Nothing directly. However, I am assuming that he nonetheless has the creation in mind. More will be said on the above later. Here, suffice it to say that Paul has Jesus with God in the beginning in thePhillipian "Christ Hymn" (2:6-7). Gen. 1:26 gives Paul some room to find a pre-existant Christ. Therein, Torah clearly reads: "Let *us* make man in our image" (ויאמר אלהים נעשה אדם בצלמנו כדמותנו). Who is the "us"—i.e., the person with God in the beginning? Paul speaks of a co-creating God who took on flesh (σάρξ), and humbled Himself (2:5-11) on the cross for us—the God-man Jesus. Paul understands that this incarnated God is to be *confessed as Lord* (2:11): He is called the Lord both explicitly (2:19; 3:8, 20) and implicitly (2:24, 29; 3:1; 4:1). What kind of relationship should the Philippian community have with this God-man? Paul encourages them to: *rejoice in Him* (3:1), *agree in Him* (4:2), *suffer for Him* (3:8), *stand firm in Him* (4:1), and *await His return* (3:20).[152]

---

[151] Interestingly אלהים ("Elohim") is used and not יהוה ("Jehovah"). The masculine suffix (ים /*im*) indicates that *this name is plural*. Paul has an answer to this mystery which he explains in his, as I want to call it here, "Incarnational Christology."

[152] James Dunn observes that Judaic "Covenantal Nomism" inevitably reinforced a sense of "separateness from other nations" (e.g., *Bar.* 3:36-4:4; *Ps. Sol.* 13:6-11; Philo. *Vit. Mos.* 2.17-25; Josephus, *Ag. Ap.* 2:38 §§277-86) and that

The Evolution of a Revolution

Again, Paul's God became incarnate (Latin, *incarnatus*). Paul understands this incarnate God, Jesus Christ (ישוע המשיח / Ἰησοῦς Χριστός) to be Israel's Messiah (cf.,1:1, 2, 6, 8, 10, 11, 13, 15, 17-21, 23, 26, 27, 29; 2:1, 5, 11, 16, 21, 30; 3:3, 7-9, 12, 14, 18, 20; 4:7, 19, 21, 23). Paul's ubiquitous usage of the predicate "Christ" itself presupposes a linkage between his Christology and his Old Testament theology—and thus "Salvation history." Those who posit that Philippians evidences no such connection in Paul's thought (cf., Dr. Hays[153] and Dr. Krentz[154]), of course, stand corrected. More will be said on the source of Paul's Christology later, and so I need not treat it extensively now.

Spirit/Ruach

Paul speaks of God's Spirit (πνεῦμα) as: a *helper* (1:19), as one who provides a means of *fellowship* (2:1), and as the *genuine vehicle for worship* (3:3). Paul knew of the Spirit's existence in advance of his existential encounter with Christ. The Torah's *Ruach Elohim* (רוח אלהים, or the Spirit of God) was "moving" at creation (cf., Gen. 1:2, ורוח אלהים מרחפת על פני המים) as was Jesus, according to Paul's Christological interpretation.[155]

Anthropomorphism and Monotheism

From the above, we can observe that Paul's *God* (יהוה), Paul's *God-Man, Messiah and/or Son* (משיח), and Paul's *Spirit* (רוח אלהים) have roots in a Jewish understanding of the protological section of the Old Testament. In follows, we'll

---

this colors much of Paul's argument in Galatians. (*Pauline Theology*, Vol. I., pp. 125-146) I see this likewise reflected in Paul's Philippian exhortation, for reasons that will be made clear below, when the "Aleynu" will be discussed.

[153] See "Crucified With Christ," *Pauline Theology*, Vol. I., p. 244.

[154] Krentz, "Tracking the Elusive Center: On Integrating Paul's Theology" (an unpublished S.B.L. paper), p. 31.

[155] The anthropomorphic activity of God becoming man was a bit innovative—perhaps; yet, *there are assorted anthropomorphic ascriptions in the intertestamental Targums* which may be cited in support of Paul's theological assertion: Jesus = a God-man (e.g., "Memra"). I thank Dr. Louis Goldberg for bringing this to my attention.

The Evolution of a Revolution

consider the Shema (שמע) in Deut. 6:4—"Hear O Israel, the Lord our God, the Lord is *one*"—and note how Paul employs, in his own way, Judaism's primary confession.

Dr. Wayne Meeks, of Yale University's Divinity school, has observed that a major boundary marker of early Christianity was the confession "One God, one Lord!"[156] (cf., 1 Cor. 8:6). To this, Oxford Professor N. T. Wright adds the following: "This confession [(i.e., the primal Christian confession)] is itself a rewriting, whether by Paul or by some other early Christian, of the Jewish confession of faith, the *Shema.*"[157] He then goes on to say that "This, in fact, I believe to be the heart of the Pauline doctrine of Justification by faith."[158] I agree!

In the Hebrew Bible, the last letter of the first word of Deut. 6:4 (the *Shema*) and the last letter of the last word in the declaration are written in larger, bolder type. (Deut. 6:4, e.g. שמע ישראל יהוה אלהינו יהוה אחד). Why? The idea is that when the Shema is read the ע and ד are brought together and then a new word/concept is birthed in the process of reading the text. Dr. J. H. Hertz, former chief rabbi of the British empire, explains: "These two large letters form the word עד [meaning] 'witness'. [Thus e]very Israelite by pronouncing the Shema becomes one of God's witnesses, *testifying to His unity before the world.*"[159] Isn't this exactly what Paul was about? Wasn't he especially interested in being a witness to the world?

Ethical Monotheism

Again, I posit that *Paul contextualized the Torah's message in order to give it a voice in the Gentile world.* For Dr. Ernst Käsemann, Paul's "Christological orientation distinguishes him from the Jewish tradition."[160] Dr. Käsemann mis-

---

[156] N. T. Wright, "Putting Paul Together Again," *Pauline Theology*, Vol. I., p. 185.
[157] *Ibid.*
[158] *Ibid.*
[159] Italics mine; Hertz, J. H., *Pentateuch and Haftorahs* (London: Soncino, 1988)), p. 770.
[160] Käsemann, E., "The Righteousness of God," *Pauline Theology*, Vol. I., p. 178.

The Evolution of a Revolution

takenly thinks that Paul is being totally innovative on this score—i.e., God's "faithfulness is in the context of the community,"[161] and that righteousness is not primarily a private, individual matter—but, it's communal."[162] Käsemann misses the fact that Paul's notion reflects a standard Jewish understanding (in fact, it's the very quintessence of a godly life). *Christian Bible scholars would be well served by distancing themselves from their historic preoccupation with insisting on seeing Paul distinguished from his day and time, and severed from his ancestral Jewish faith and practice.*

In sum, Paul's understanding of God's person and will is formulated, in part, by a subtextual Jewish hermeneutic that finds logical expression, for Paul, in the incarnated Jesus Christ—the Messiah.[163] Paul's God became an ordinary man, to deal with contemporary man. If God can do it, so can Paul! Likewise, Paul's (Jewish) message took on ordinary human (Gentile) expression in order to deal with all humanity—both Jews and Greeks, slave and free, and male and female.

How Modern Theologians Understand Paul

This subsection will explore what other religious thinkers are saying about Paul's incarnational theology, by examining what I call: *Context: Messianism as Matrix,* and then *Text: Messianic Hymn as Metaphor.* By "context" I am referring to the background that informs the Philippian letter; by "text" I

---

[161] *Ibid.*, 174.

[162] *Ibid.*, p. 176. Stowers calls this "horatory psychogogic"—i.e., moving from isolated individualization toward a functioning community (Stowers, *Op. Cit.*, pp. 107-114).

[163] This is what some Christian theologians want to call a "cruciform." One need only look at the *Decalogue* and observe how the first five "commands" deal with the vertical dimension—man and God; secondly, one need but briefly refer to the next five and see how they speak to a horizontal plane—man and man. Judaism has always understood that righteouness relates to working within a community and not departing from it to opt for an individualistic, introspective existence. Hays refers to the cruciform as the "normative paradigm for all Christian believers now" (p. 241). Of course, Paul isn't really saying anything new; rather, *he's inventing a way to say it to Gentiles* (see below).

The Evolution of a Revolution

am referring to the *locus classicus* of the correspondence—a redacted Jewish prayer, today called the "Christ Hymn."

Context: Messianism as Matrix

Previously we heard Professor Geza Vermes say that "We will not get the revival of scholarship that we look for until interpreters of the Christian gospels learn to *immerse themselves in the native religion of Jesus the Jew, and in the general climate of the world and age in which he lived.*"[164] I referred to him, Dr. Sanders,[165] and Dr. Charlesworth[166] to demonstrate that there is indeed an appreciation for Jewish Studies in Christian circles, in general; now, let's see if it's discernible in Pauline theology in Philippians, in particular.

Dr. N. T. Wright, at Oxford, believes, as I, that *Paul's theology is a redefinition of Jewish doctrines of monotheism and election, by means of Christology.* This then corresponds to Dr. J. Christiaan Beker's—an expert on Pauline thought and professor at Princeton—analysis of Pauline eschatology, which according to both Beker and Wright is informed by *Paul's radical and startling Christological redefinition.*[167]

Casually, Dr. Stanley Stowers asserts that Paul must be read from "Jewish and early Christian codes," but he doesn't have much more to say on the matter. Likewise, Dr. David Lull observes how Paul's "symbolic world" is made up of traditions from post-Biblical Judaism and the non-Jewish Greco-Roman world, as well as Jewish and pagan philosophers[168]; but he, like Dr. Stowers, does not seem very interested in pursuing the implications—at least not to my satisfaction.

It has been observed that Paul breaks with the Old Testa-

---

[164] Italics mine; Vermes, G., *Jesus and the World of Judaism* (Philadelphia: Fortress Press, 1984), p. 73.
[165] Sanders, E. P., *Jesus and Judaism* (Philadelphia: Fortress Press, 1985).
[166] Charlesworth, J., *Jesus Within Judaism* (New York: Doubleday, 1988).
[167] Wright, *Op. Cit.*, p. 184, 189-190.
[168] Lull, D., "Salvation History," *Pauline Theology*, Vol. I., p. 249.

The Evolution of a Revolution

ment tradition. Dr. Edgar Krentz mistakenly asserts: "Paul never cites the Old Testament explicitly in Philippians, nor does he refer to any Old Testament personage, institution (except for 3:3, 5), in short, *the Old Testament is not a warrant for anything that Paul holds in Philippians.*"[169] I certainly do not agree with Dr, Krentz! Dr. John Reumann notes the absence of direct Old Testament quotations in the text, but he doesn't go so far as to make the same mistake that Krentz does. Reumann observes: "[There is] nothing said [in Philippians] about a divine role in creation... though many characteristics [of the general text] fit with the Old Testament depiction of Yahweh."[170] Reumann will at least recognize that there are characteristics of Old Testament theology reflected in Philippians; Krentz shuts the door on the possibilities—and mind you, *he'll be the worse off for having done so!* "Missing from Philippians," observes Dr. Stowers, "is any form of a later orthodox narrative of salvation, that is, the view that humans have an ontological and/or moral flaw due to a primordial fall that only the incarnation or the substitutional sacrifice of an adequate offering for sin can erase."[171] No creation account. No offering for sin. No Old Testament!!! Has Paul totally abandoned his Jewish roots? I think not!

Once again, we turn to Professor N. T. Wright who firmly asserts: "[We must reject the view that Paul] "abandoned Judaism as such... [Paul's fidelity is reflected through his belief that] the true interpretation of the covenant with Abraham was the Christian, worldwide family-characterized-by-faith."[172] Paul's new/true interpretation of the "covenant" called for a *revised Old Testament theology, not a displacement of it.* Dr. Richard Hays argues this point saying:

---

[169] Krentz, E., *Op. Cit.*, p. 31.

[170] Reusmann, J., "The Theologies of 1 Thessalonians and Philippians: Contents, Comparison and Composite," S.B.L. Seminar Papers, 1987, p. 533.

[171] Stowers, *Op. Cit.*, p. 120.

[172] *Ibid.*, p. 210.

The Evolution of a Revolution

"God's act in Jesus Christ illuminates a previously uncomprehended narrative unity in scripture. It turns out, according to Paul, that scripture from the first was always about God's intention to bless the Gentiles through Christ."[173] Dr. David Lull, in his own way, concurs: "Paul transfers the characteristics and attributes of Israel as the people of God to the mixed Christian community of Gentiles and Jews."[174]

Emphatically, Dr. Wright argues—and we'll let his challenge bring closure to this section on "context"—that we *must* "grapple with the task of understanding Paul's own thought forms and thought patterns as a Pharisee and then as a Christian, and attempt to restate them coherently in such a way as to show their proper interrelation within a total worldview without doing voilence en route."[175]

Text: Messianic Hymn as Metaphor

In what follows, I shall attempt what Dr. Wright suggests. This I'll do through an examination of Philippians 2:5-11—the epistle's governing metaphor. To understand the locus of the letter, we'll: (1) first examine Paul's contingent situation in brief; (2) then we'll engage in a cursory examination of the letter's coherent center—wherein we'll hopefully see how all the theological roads lead both to 2:5-11 and from it.

Contingent Situation

As was previously noted, Paul was helped by the Philippian community in various ways, and this correspondence was his way of saying thanks. As of this writing, Paul is imprisoned and awaiting trial for his life. Against this backdrop, he provides us with a sober view of Christian life and Christian death. His affliction for the "cause of his Gospel" caused him to reflect on his exemplar—Jesus Christ, who gave His life for

---

[173] Hays., R., "Crucifed With Christ," *Pauline Theology*, Vol. I., p. 237.
[174] Lull, D., *Op. Cit.*, p. 248.
[175] Wright, *Op. Cit.*, p. 197.

The Evolution of a Revolution

Paul and for all. For this reason, Phil. 2:5-11, a pericope detailing God's self-emptying, is of prime importance for Paul, as well as for those of us who wish to inquire into the specifics of Paul's view of God.

Coherent Center
General Overview of the Philippian Text

Dr. Charles Ryrie outlines the Philippians text[176] as follows: I. 1:1-11, Greetings and Expressions of Gratitude; II. 1:12-30, Paul's Personal [Difficult] Circumstances; III. 2:1-30, The Pattern of the Christian Life: The Humility of Christ; IV. 3:1-21, The Prize of the Christian Life; and lastly V. 4:1-23, The Peace of the Christian Life.[177]

It seems to me that a scarlet thread running through the text isn't hard to find. Paul writes his "friendly"[178] letter (1:3-11) expressing his appreciation for them as well as his confidence that God's hand is active in his own dilemma (1:12-30). Paul redacts a Jewish hymn by giving it a Christological gloss (see below) (2:1-11) for his Gentile audience. Mindful of his exemplar (Jesus), he expresses his own willingness to "pour himself out as an offering,"[179] and he then encourages the community likewise (2:12-18). He then boasts of Timothy and

---

[176] I'm aware that textual critics have located, what they believe to be, three texts in this correspondence, e.g., Reusmann, p. 528 and Perkins, pp. 89-90. Herein, I prefer to simply sidestep the matter: it's agreed, as I understand it, that Paul wrote all three texts—if three is what's preferred. Consequently, *I'm confident that I'm working with Paul's thought* irrespective of how one deals with the objection to a single text. Furthermore, herein I'm really only seriously concerned with one pericope 2:5-11 and there's no reason to believe that it stands at the crossroads between any two or three texts.

[177] Ryrie, C., *The Ryrie Study Bible* (Chicago: Moody Press, 1978), p. 1682.

[178] Though not treated in this chapter, I'd like to acknowledge a certain indebtedness to Dr. Stanley Stowers for his excellent unpacking of the letter's "friendship theme" (Stowers, pp. 107-114).

[179] Pagans had assorted ritual offeings, libations, etc. There's no reason to require a reference to the Old Testament cult centered in Jerusalem for this particular text; yet, it would seem likely that this is what he was thinking. He perhaps thought one way—*as a Jew*, while knowing that his audience would interpret his point as a reference to a non-Jewish practice. The result would be the same here.

The Evolution of a Revolution

Epaphroditus, men who have put their own lives on the line for the Gospel (2:19-30, esp. Timothy in 20, 21-22; Epaphroditus in 29-30). Following his constructive upbuilding, he warns about destructive ambassadors for Christ (3:1-4a). These perfidious men have nothing that Paul didn't acquire (3:4a-6) and later give away for Christ's sake, who gave Himself away for our sake (3:7-11). Mindful of Christ's giving of Himself (i.e., of Christ's humility), Paul "presses on" and encourages the community to do likewise (3:12-21). Lastly, Paul gives final exhortations to both individuals and the general community (4:1-9); he closes thanking them for their kindness which they'd extended toward him throughout his ministry (4:10-23).

The Christ Hymn and Modern Scholarship

As has been stated above, the "Christ Hymn" (so called)—really a borrowed and redacted Jewish hymn—is the locus classicus for Paul's thought in Philippians. After reading the text afresh, below, we'll proceed to examine it in the remainder of this section and the next, illuminated by the flashlights of modern scholarship—but, again, before turning the wild dogs loose on the sacred writ, let's reacquaint ourselves with it.

> 5 Let this mind be in you, which was also in Christ Jesus: 6 Who, being in the form of God, thought it not robbery to be equal with God: 7 But [he] made himself of no reputation, and took upon him the form of a servant, and was made in the likeness of men: 8 And being found in fashion as a man, he humbled himself, and became obedient unto death, even the death of the cross. 9 Wherefore God also hath highly exalted him, and given him a name which is above every name: 10 That at the name of Jesus every knee should bow, of things in heaven, and things in earth, and things under the earth; 11 And that every tongue should confess that Jesus Christ is Lord, to the glory of God the Father.

The Evolution of a Revolution

In his *New Testament Theology*, Dr. Donald Guthrie notes that there exists a controversy over the origin of the "Christ Hymn." He doesn't side, one way or the other; rather, he simply reports that: some see a "Jewish background," some a "Hellenestic," and others a "syncretism of the two."[180] Dr. Guthrie maintains that Paul could indeed have put pen to paper without the knowledge of any other similar text,[181] and goes so far as to say that the maintenance of a "pre-Pauline hymn" is "faced with more difficulties" than anything.[182] Over and against those who opt for a "Gnostic redeemer myth,"[183] Dr. Guthrie sees a connection to the "Suffering Servant" in Isaiah,[184] who is likewise exalted following his sacrificial humiliation (Isa. 53:1-12). Picking up on exaltation, Dr. Oscar Cullman sees 2:6-11 as an early "confessional formula"[185] attesting to Jesus' exalted Lordship, but he doesn't say much more than that.

Dr. Pheme Perkins opines: "Philippians 2:6-11 is taken from a pre-Pauline hymn, which the apostle has glossed and used as a central piece for his exhortation to the Philippians."[186] Dr. John Reumann agrees with Perkins saying: the "Christ Hymn" assumes a "pre-Pauline [text] used in [Jewish synagogal] worship, redacted by Paul [for his innovative "Christian" purposes], and employed for ethical purposes here."[187] What might that text have been?

Dr. John Turner, in "Sethian Gnosticism: A Literary

---

[180] Guthrie, D., *New Testament Theology* (Downers Grove: IVP, 1981), p. 345.

[181] *Ibid.*, p. 344.

[182] *Ibid.*, p. 345.

[183] *Ibid.*, pp. 346-349. In this regard *Nag Hammadi, Gnosticism, and Early Christianity*, ed. Hedrick, C. W., and Hodgson, R. (Peabody: Hendrickson Pub., 1986), can be quite helpful. The text grew out of the 1983 seminar on Gnosticism and Early Christianity.

[184] *Ibid.*, p. 265.

[185] Cullman, O., *Early Christian Worship* (Bristol: Wyndham Hall Press), p. 22.

[186] Perkins, *Op. Cit.*, pp. 91-92.

[187] Reusmann, *Op. Cit.*, p. 529.

The Evolution of a Revolution

History," observes in assorted Sethian treatises and mythologumena (e.g., *Gos. Eg.* III, 2, pp. 66-67; *Apoc. Adam* V, 5, pp. 78-82; *Melch.* XI, 1, pp. 5-6, 18-18) the following: "These materials seem to envision the descent of the savior into the world, corresponding to the descent of the king"; following his descent there's an "enthronement and exaltation of the king, priest, or priest-king."[188] Dr. Turner goes on to speak of Sethian Gnostic myths of descending (humiliation) and ascending (exaltation) figures, e.g., *Allogenes*, *Three Steeles of Seth* and *Zostrianos*. The fact that the above myths were played out against a baptismal motif suggests, to Turner, a possible similar purpose for the hymn which is the object of our present inquiry. I see other souces for the "Christ Hymn."

Dr. Richard Longnecker, in *The Christology of Early Jewish Christianity*, has a subsection entitled "The Κατάβασις and ἀνάβασις Theme," wherein he takes up the Gnostic question posed above.[189] Let's consider what he says and note why he's inclined to disagree with Turner, that the Gnostic mythologumena can serve a source for Pauline thought. First, asserts Dr. Longnecker, the Κατάβασις (ascending) and ἀνάβασις (descending) themes are by no means unique to Gnostic literature. He sees a prototype in pre-Pauline Jewish literature (e.g., *I Enoch*, 12-16) and concludes that the hymn took form originally in Palestine and should be traced to early strands of Jewish-Christianity. In sum, Longnecker sees Paul employing an early Jewish-Christian hymn in Philippians.[190] Professor Longnecker's primary concern in his treatment of the text is refuting the belief that the hymn developed in a "Hellenistic ideological milieu, and was foreign to early Palestinian Christianity"—ideas advanced by Dr. R. Bultmann and Dr. R. H. Fuller, to name but a few.[191] Dr. Longnecker wants nothing to

---

[188] Turner, *Nag Hammadi, Gnosticism, and Early Christianity*, p. 69.
[189] Longnecker, R., *The Christology of Early Jewish Christianity* (Grand Rapids: Baker, 1981), pp. 58-62.
[190] *Ibid.*

-123-

The Evolution of a Revolution

do with Pauline theology rooted in a myth! Instead, he argues that the song speaks of "[Christ's] adoration as based upon the facts of his humiliation and death."[192]

Dr. Robert Lightner sees an apocalyptic vindication, as do I, at the hymn's close, when Paul speaks of *all* "knees bowing" and *every* "tongue confessing" the "name" of Jesus one day—thus eventually, it will be apparent to all that Jesus is all He claimed to be, Christ the King.[193] Dr. H. A. Kennedy suggests that through exalting "the Name," "perhaps the apostle has in his mind the Jewish use of הַשֵׁם [i.e.] "the Name," as a reverant substitute for יהוה (LXX, Κύριος).[194] Immediately then, leaning on Dr. Jeremy Taylor (*Works*, Vol. II., p. 72), Kennedy makes a point that brings us back to the starting point here—i.e., the incarnational aspect of Paul's theologizing: "He hath changed the ineffable name into a name utterable by man, and desirable by all the world; the majesty is all arrayed in robes of mercy, the tetragrammaton or adorable mystery of the patriarchs is made fit for pronunciation and expression when it becomes the name of the Lord's Christ."[195]

Paul envisions a triumphal climax in history when *every* knee bows to a Jewish king, Jesus—and that includes Gentile knees; *every* tongue confesses Jesus' lordship—and that includes Jewish tongues. Truly, herein we observe the apostle's innovative and creative genius! What profundity! What vision! What an adoption of a Jewish theme! With this in mind, we'll close with Dr. Krister Stendahl, former Dean of Harvard Divinity school, who posited that, working within a primarily Gentile milieu, Paul nevertheless worked from a primarily Jewish apocalyptic matrix: *"There's a triumphal-*

---

[191] *Ibid.*, pp. 60-61.

[192] *Ibid.*, p. 103.

[193] *Bible Knowledge Commentary*, Vol. II., ed. Walvoord & Zuck (Wheaton: Victor Books, 1984), pp. 654-655.

[194] *The Expositor's Greek New Testament*, Vol. III., ed. W. R. Nicoll (Grand Rapids: Eerdmans, 1988), p. 438.

[195] *Ibid.*, p. 439.

ism in Paul's salvation history, it is a Jewish triumphalism—to be sure a Jewish-Christian triumphalism, but a Jewish one nevertheless."[196]

How Jewish Theology Enables Us to Get at the Root of Pauline Theology

Dr. Philip Segal delivered a paper to the Annual Conference of the Studiorium Novi Testamenti Societas, entitled "Early Christian and Rabbinic Liturgical Affinities: Exploring Liturgical Acculturation."[197] He prefaces his work observing that early Christian liturgy was "Judaic in both structure and content although now and then reconstituted in a hellenistic-christological manner."[198] Segal sees Jewish acculturation in early Jewish-Christian *piyyutim*. Known by ποιητής to Greek speakers and פיט to Hebrew ones, *Piyyutim*, are lyrical compositions intended to embellish obligatory prayers.[199] Dr. Segal sees affinities between the evolving corpi of Christian and rabbinical Jewish liturgical material. He investigates assorted early "Christian" texts for affinities to "Jewish" faith and practice, e.g., *Didascalia, Apostolic Tradition of Hippolytus, Apostolic Constitutions, Didache, Epistle of Barnabas* and Pseudo-Clementine literature,[200] and then devotes an entire section to the "Christ Hymn," which he entitles "Phil. 2:10-11 and Aleynu."[201]

Though it's uncertain as to exactly who first composed this liturgical hymn, it's generally understood to have originated

---

[196] Italics mine. Lull, D., *Op. Cit.*, p. 252; from Stendahl, K., *Paul Among Jews and Gentiles and Other Essays* (Philadelphia: Fortress Press, 1976), pp. 131-132.

[197] Delivered on August 27th, 1980; cf. Segal, P., in *New Test. Stud.*, vol. 30, pp. 63-90.

[198] *Ibid.*, p. 63.

[199] See *Encyclopedia Judaica*, Vol. 13 (Jerusalem: Keter Publishing, 1971), pp. 573-602.

[200] Segal, *Op. Cit.*, pp. 64-69.

[201] Käsemann rejects there being a Jewish connection between the Christ Hymn and the Aleynu; instead, he opts for a Hellenistic Gnostic myth (*Ibid.*, p. 76).

The Evolution of a Revolution

during the inter-testamental period, against the backdrop of hellenistic encroachment. With the threat of assimilation and/or annihilation, the "Aleynu" (עלינו) was composed; and subsequently it came to serve as a Jewish confessional statement, which it is to this very day.

In evidence of the above, we will look again at the conclusion of Paul's "Christ Hymn" and then at the "Aleynu." See if you can detect any similarities between Christ's triumphal reign, following His humiliation, and what's envisioned for Israel, in regard to her eventual vindication over the oppressing heathen.

> **Philippians 2:9-11**
> 9 Wherefore God also hath highly exalted him, and given him a name which is above every name: 10 That at the name of Jesus every knee should bow, of things in heaven, and things in earth, and things under the earth; 11 And that every tongue should confess that Jesus Christ is Lord, to the glory of God the Father.

With Paul's words still in our ears, let us now consider the following Jewish prayer.

> **The Aleynu**
> [1.] It is for us to praise the Lord of all things, to acclaim the author of all existence. [a.] He did not make us like the heathen of the earth; [b.] He did not fashion us like the pagans of the world. [c.] Our portion is not like theirs, our lot is not like that of their multitudes.
> 　[2.] We bend the knee, bow down, and acclaim the supreme King of Kings, the Holy One, praised be He. [3.] It is He who stretched forth the heavens and laid the foundations of the earth. [a.] His glorious presence is in the heavens above, the dominion of His might is in the loftiest heights. [b.] He is our God; there is none else. [c.] He is our King; there is none other. [d.] As it is

The Evolution of a Revolution

written in His Torah: and you shall know this day and meditate in your heart, that the Lord is Master in the heavens above and on the earth beneath. [e.] There is none else.

[4.] We therefore hope in Thee O Lord of God, that we shall soon behold the triumph of Thy might, when idolatry will be uprooted from the earth and falsehood will utterly be destroyed. [5.] We hope for the day when the world will be perfected under the dominion of the Almighty and all mankind learn to revere Thy name; when all the wicked of the earth will be drawn into penitence unto Thee.

[6.] O may all the inhabitants of the earth recognize that unto Thee every knee must bend, every tongue pledge loyalty. [7.] Before Thee, O Lord our God, may they bow down in worship, and give honor to Thy glorious name. [8.] May they all acknowledge Thy kingdom, and may Thy dominion be established over them speedily and forevermore. [a.] For sovereignty is Thine and unto all eternity Thou wilt reign in glory. [9.] As is written in Torah: The Lord will reign forever and ever. [a.] And it is further written: The Lord will be acknowledged as King over all the earth; on that day will the Lord be One and His name One.

Analysis of the Jewish Text

With a vision of a future exaltation for God and vindication for Israel, the covenant people are encouraged by the "Aleynu" to live proleptically—i.e., as though the believed for future was already here. Jehovah, the God of Israel, is in reality the Lord of *all* creation—though only Israel knows it at present. Jews, who are unlike the Gentiles, must carry the standard—the Torah; Jews are persecuted for doing so. God is faithful; He will vindicate His people when He vindicates His name.

In the meantime, Israel is encouraged to "praise the Lord" (v. 1). The oppressing heathen don't know God—nor are they known by Him at present (v. 1 a-b). In contradistinction, Israel

The Evolution of a Revolution

does know Him, and bows to Him only (v. 2). Jehovah created this present order, and so He and He only is worthy of praise (v. 3 a-e).

Israel's psalms of praise to their King of Kings, no doubt, may lack vitality owing to the fact that He had seemingly been beaten by the pagan deities in battle. His Name "Jehovah" (i.e., "I Am") may indeed seem inappropriate; better would read a name like "I Was." Where is their King? Where is their God? When will He show himself victorious over His/Israel's enemies? When will the vindication come?

Mindful of vv. 1-3, Israel is encouraged to hope in the eventual triumph of the Lord: "We therefore hope in Thee, O Lord our God, that we might soon behold the triumph of Thy might, when idolatry will be uprooted from the earth and falsehood will be utterly destroyed" (v. 4). Of course, against the might of the heathen, Israel can do little more than "hope" for an eventual triumph and take solace in a dream that, one day, the world will be, as the song goes, "perfected under the dominion of the Almighty and *all mankind learn to revere Thy name; when all the wicked of the earth will be drawn into penitence unto Thee* (v. 5). What's of special interest here is the theme of *global* regeneration—*all* the earth's wicked are drawn to Judaism's "King of Kings." *This includes Gentiles.*

The song's theme—i.e., God's vindication and triumph over His created order, resulting in a transnational acknowledgment of His sovereignty—is reiterated in even stronger terms as we progress through the text. "O may all the inhabitants of the earth recognize that unto Thee every knee must bend, every tongue pledge loyalty. Before Thee, O Lord our God, may they bow down in worship, and give honor to Thy glorious name. May they all acknowledge Thy kingdom, and may Thy dominion be established over them speedly and forevermore. For sovereignty is Thine and unto all eternity Thou wilt reign in glory. As is written in Torah: The Lord will reign forever and ever.

The Evolution of a Revolution

And it is further written: The Lord will be acknowledged as King over all the earth; on that day will the Lord be One and His name One" (vv. 6-9a).

Much like the "Lord's Prayer," the "Aleynu" is likely informed by assorted Old Testament texts, e.g., cf., Isa. 30:7; 45:20-23; Deut. 4:39; Ex. 15:18; Zech. 14:9;[202] but for our purposes we need only refer to one, Isa. 45:20-23, wherein we can observe the following: v. 20 = against pagan worship; v. 21 = affirmation of only one God; v. 22 = appeal for global repentance (cf., "turn to me and be saved *all the ends of the earth*") and acknowledgment of the one true God (cf., "For I am God and there is no other"); and v. 23 = "To me every knee shall bow, every tongue shall swear." Clearly, Isaiah 45:20-23 informs the "Aleynu"; and clearly, the "Aleynu" informs the "Christ Hymn," the locus for Pauline theology in his letter to the Philippian community.

Comparing the "Aleynu" and the "Christ Hymn"

Paul, in a Roman prison and at risk of loosing limb and/or life, remembers the *piyyot* that best articulates Israel's struggle with the Greeks. With authors and audiences hard pressed on every side, from without and from within, the "Aleynu" and the "Christ Hymn" both look beyond the dismal circumstances to the Messianic Era. Both envision God's eventual exaltation over oppressing heathen. The "Aleynu" has a *hope*; however, it lacks a program—it manages to articulate the future, but fails to explicate the particulars. From Paul's viewpoint, *Judaism's hope needs but one thing, and one thing only—a Christ event, a catalyst for the age to come!* Paul has discovered Israel's/Torah's answer: Jesus the Messiah—the incarnated "Word become flesh"; he has also recovered Israel's mission in the process—i.e., that of being a "light to all the nations." The locus for Paul's incarnational theologizing, in Philippians, is a Jewish hymn built on the

---
[202] Segal, *Op. Cit.*, p. 76.

The Evolution of a Revolution

foundation of Isaiah 45: 18-25.[203]

Summary & Conclusion

In short, I believe that Paul's fluid theological thought-world was fueled by a subtextual Messianic Jewish matrix,[204] culminating in the Christ event.[205] Jewish apocalyptic thought—i.e., the realization of Israel's prophetic destiny—more than anything else, provides a foundation for understanding Paul's views. At times, Paul masked the Hebraic origin of his message, owing to assorted contingent situations he happened upon in his Gentile mission—his audience didn't really require a Jewish reading; however, it was never hidden from Paul. As evidenced by the "Christ Hymn," *Paul—the Apostle to the Gentiles—was about the business of Israel's hope, and was informed by an incarnational approach to Jewish Scripture and Israel's mission.*

The upshot of the above, I believe, is that we are forced to the conclusion that though Paul's innovative contextualization evidences the movement's evolution from its Jewish to Greek forms, we're best served by remembering that the new Pauline form itself was still fundamentally Jewish. Others, as we shall see, lost sight of this altogether.

---

[203] Special thanks to Mr. Steve Cohen, a ThM student, at the time, at Dallas Theological Seminary, who encouraged me to clarify the connection between the "Aleynu" and the "Christ Hymn."

[204] J. Christiaan Beker speaks of a fluid coherent center of Pauline theology located in the sub-textual level of the Pauline corpus. (See *The Triumph of God* [Minneapolis: Fortress Press, 1990], p. 134.) I agree with Beker, for reasons that should be clear by now.

[205] Cf., N. T. Wright's usage in "Putting Paul Together," *Pauline Theology*, Vol. I., ed. J. M. Bassler (Minneapolis: Fortress, 1991), pp. 190-195: he says the task is to get *behind* Pauls rationalization(s), to the convictions that inform them (p. 192-193). I, of course, agree.

III

Case Studies on the Christian Re-Interpretation of Sacred Scripture and Sacred Space

Introduction

This chapter is 400+ years removed from Paul and the Judean world of chapter II—quite a leap, I realize. The ancient Judean/Greco-Roman world changed considerably over the many centuries and *both* Christians and Jews were affected and effected. As you may recall, chapter II was about Christians *and* Jews—the accent marks being on the connection between them; this chapter is likewise about Christians *and* Jews— *the accents, here, however are on their disconnection.* Here, in the Roman Christian period, it's Christians *against* Jews.

Latin or Roman Christianity, owing to the incredible turn of events in the early fourth century, understood itself to have totally taken over Israel's place in God's economy—a theological understanding that has endured over time. Armed with this (mis)understanding, Latin churchmen reinterpreted "Jewish" biblical literature, to service their own "Catholic" need to ground their "triumph" in Holy Writ's prophetic utterances. This chapter—divided into two subsections: (1) "The Roman Christian Re-Interpretation of Judaism's Sacred Scripture" and (2) "The Roman Christian Re-Interpretation of Judaism's Sacred Space"—concerns itself with noting this , and more.

The Evolution of a Revolution

A. The Christian Re-Interpretation of Judaism's Sacred Scripture

Theology & History: Explaining Unprecedented Events in a Rapidly Changing World

History From a Christian Vantage Point

St. Augustine (354-430) entered the stage of the human drama at a time of change for both state and church. Initially a republic guided by an astute senate and carefully watched by a patricio-plebian aristocracy, the Romans felt the call of destiny. Following the long Punic Wars, northern Africa was secured; thus Rome controlled the Mediterranean sea (they called it *mare nostrum*—i.e., "Our Sea") and the world around it. Under Julius Caesar, Africa was systematically Latinized. Though she held her torch high for a season, Rome's fire eventually burnt out.

St. Augustine was born at a time when Rome had passed her prime: the Senate's power was virtually gone; the army, or sections of it, were out of control—they'd proclaimed emperors frequently; the empire had lost its grip, and people had lost confidence in it. Diocletian sought to rejuvenate the empire through an autocratic rule that extended through Constantine and his heirs[206]; initially there was excitement, as a converted "Christian" Rome brought hopes of a return to her former glory, but this was short lived and replaced with pessimism.

As was St. Augustine's state, his church was likewise undergoing a metamorphosis. In the fourth century, the persecuted[207] Christian ἐκκλησία had been transformed into the predicted victorious ישראל (Israel) envisioned in the Old Testament.[208] Dr. Jacob Neusner quotes Dr. J. N. D. Kelly, who

---

[206] Warren Thomas Smith, "Augustine's World," *Augustine: His Life and Thought* (Atlanta: John Knox Press, 1980), pp. 1-6.

[207] From 303-311, emperor Diocletian Galerius launched what was the worst of the ten waves of persecution against the church. Churches and Bibles were destroyed; all civil rights were suspended; sacrifice to gods was mandatory (see Robert Walton's *Chronological and Background Charts of Church History* [Grand Rapids: Zondervan/Academie Books, 1986], p. 10).

The Evolution of a Revolution

observed: "At the beginning of the century [the Church] had been reeling under a violent persecution... Now it found itself showered with benefactions and privileges, invited to undertake responsibilities, and progressively given a directive role in society."[209]

The euphoria served to intoxicate many churchmen, some of whom, noted Dr. Erwin R. Goodenough, "...would begin to dream of itself [i.e., the Church, as] being the ideal rulership for the world."[210] Eusebius evidences this trend in the way he began his account of the revolutionary age of Constantine. Worthy of note for our purposes here is how the Christian conquest, spiritual and material, of Gentile Rome was understood by the ancient historiographer, Eusebius,[211] to be a fulfillment of prophetic "ancient declarations"—i.e., Hebrew Scripture.[212] He says:

> [Not] by hearsay merely or report, but [we] observe... in very deed and with our own eyes that *the declarations recorded long ago are faithful and true...* 'as we have heard, so we have seen, in the city of the Lord of hosts, in the city of our God.' And in what city but in the newly built and god-constructed one, which is a 'church of the living God'....[213]

---

[208] See Robert Markus "Holy Places and Holy People," in *The End of Ancient Christianity* (Cambridge: Cambridge University Press, 1990), pp. 139-155.

[209] *Jerome: His Life and His Teachings* (New York: Harper & Row, 1975), pp. 1-2; in Jacob Neusner, *Judaism and Christianity in the Age of Constantine*, p. 15.

[210] *The Church in the Roman Empire* (New York: Henry Holt, 1932; reproduced in New York by Cooper Square Publishers); from Jacob Neusner, *Judaism and Christianity in the Age of Constantine*, p. 16.

[211] St. Augustine was a bit more sober minded than Eusebius. He *didn't* have an over inflated view of earthly government; instead he set his sights towards the eschaton (the world to come) when humanity would enjoy perfect social order and genuine felicity.

[212] E.g., the prophets of old had envisioned a time when "the earth would be filled with the knowledge of the Lord as the waters cover the sea" Isa. 11:9b—a prophecy understood to be being fulfilled in St. Augustine's day.

The Evolution of a Revolution

Elsewhere, Eusebius again asserts:

> [O]ur life and our conduct, with our doctrines of religion, have not been lately invented by us, but from the first creation of man... have been established by the natural understanding of divinely favored men of old.[214]

Endeavoring to tell the history of pagan Rome with Jewish Scripture was indeed quite innovative; and the attempt brought with it a host of new problems. How does one take the incredible "Jewish" sacred writings—the works Eusebius called of "divinely favored men of old"—and make them credible for a primarily "Gentile" Greco-Roman audience? Once the *how* is answered, it remains to determine *who* will rise to form the new dogma. Dr. Arnaldo Momigliano proves very insightful in explaining the situation:

> The new history could not suppress the old. Adam and Eve and what follows had in some way to be presented in a world populated by Deucalion, Cadmus, Romulus and Alexander the Great. This created all sorts of new problems. First, the pagans had to be introduced to the Jewish version of history. Secondly, the Christian historians were expected to silence the objection that Christianity was new.... Thirdly, the pagan facts of life had to get into the Jewish-Christian scheme of redemption... It soon became imperative for the Christians to produce a chronology which would satisfy both the needs of the elementary teaching and the purposes of higher historical interpretation....

---

[213] Italics mine; *Church History*, trans. Arthur Cushman McGiffert, in *Select Library of the Nicene and Post-Nicene Fathers of the Christian Church*, ed. Philip Schaaf and Henry Wace (Grand Rapids: Eerdmans), p. 369; gleaned from Jacob Neusner, *Judaism and Christianity in the Age of Constantine*, p. 30.

[214] *Church History* (1:4), *Ibid.*, p. 33.

The Evolution of a Revolution

Christian chronology was also a philosophy of history.[215]

St. Augustine rose to the occasion and provided a theological explication that answered to the above mentioned criteria. He brought together: "the revelation of the Bible, the wisdom of Greek philosophy and the honour and dignity of her own [religious] tradition, and so enabl[ed] members of her [Gentile] church to enter the Eternal City of Heaven...."[216] As bishop, he was the bridge between various worlds: Biblical and classical Greek, as well as the collapsing imperial Roman world and the emerging new spiritual society.[217]

History from a Jewish Vantage Point

For centuries, Judaism's religious leaders were trained in the *Mishnah*, a text concerned with a limited sphere of Jewish religious jurisprudence.[218] Though limited to matters of triviality (e.g., who could marry and divorce, etc.), Judaism's rabbis (little more than minor bureaucrats) still had a certain minuscule measure of authority. These clerks were appointed by Jewish patriarchs until the patriarchate came to an end in 429 when the emperor refused to appoint a new one, owing to a

---

[215] Arnaldo Momigliano "Pagan and Christian Historiography in the Fourth Century," in *The Conflict Between Christianity and Paganism in the Fourth Century* (Oxford: Clarendon Press, 1963), p. 81; gleaned from Jacob Neusner, *Judaism and Christianity in the Age of Constantine*, p. 33.

[216] *City of God*, trans. Henry Bettenson, rear cover.

[217] See Christopher Dawson's essay "St. Augustine and His Age" (i) "The Dying World," in *St. Augustine: His Age, His Life and Thought* (New York: Meridian Books, 1957), p. 15, p. 33.

[218] The *Mishna* (משנה: "to repeat, learn or teach") is a compilation of Jewish religious law broken down into the following six divisions: (1) *Zeraim* זרעים: "Seeds," dealing with agricultural laws; (2) *Moed* מועד: "Appointed Times," festivals and feasts; (3) *Nashim* נשים: "Women," marriage, divorce, vows; (4) *Nezikin* נזיקין: "Damages," civil and criminal law; (5) *Kodoshim* קדשים: "Holy Things," Temple rituals; (6) *Taharot* טהרות:"Purity," laws of ritual purity and impurity. It along with its amplifications in the *Gemara* (גמרא: "to accomplish, learn or study") constitute the bulk of Jewish halacha, called the *Talmud* (תלמוד: "the studying or the teaching").

The Evolution of a Revolution

systematic Christian-initiated attempt to subjugate Judaism.[219]

What hope would there be for Judaism in a world that was increasingly hostile? The regnant nation (Christianity) was an ancient rival but now Judaism's master, owing to a strange turn of events. *Christianity's sudden rise in the empire was accompanied by Judaism's systematic demise.* Against the backdrop of a changing world system—one that, for Judaism, was changing for the *worse*—the rabbis were forced to answer some pressing questions: *What* is happening? *Why* is it happening? *When* is it going to stop happening? *How* will it stop happening? To answer these—all related to God's action in history—the sages needed some help.

The Mishnah had been their source of instruction for minor civil and religious affairs, but *it didn't concern itself with history*; to the contrary, it avoided it. In late antiquity, the sages could no longer afford to avoid the world. Providing another example of how "necessity is the mother of invention," Judaism's sages turned to the Holy Books to search afresh for God's word for their circumstances. Assorted Midrashim[220] were the fruits of their labors. Dr. Jacob Neusner explains:

> The first of these books of exegesis were brought to closure, it is universally agreed, in the fifth and sixth centuries of the Common Era (C.E.) in the

---

[219] Jacob Neusner put it well: "In the beginning of the fourth century Rome was pagan; by the end of the century it was Christian. In the beginning [of the century] Jews in the land of Israel administered their own affairs. In the end, their institution of self-administration lost the recognition it had formerly enjoyed" (see *Judaism and Christianity in the Age of Constantine*, p. 17).

[220] *Midrash* (מדרש) comes from the word *darash* (דרש) meaning "to inquire" to "investigate" (see Ben Isaacson, *Dictionary of the Jewish Religion* [Englewood, NJ: SBS Publishers, with Bantam Books, Inc., 1979], p. 116). In some ways these compilations are akin to the Apocrypha (ἀπόκρυφος: "hidden or concealed") and the later *Kabbalah* (קבלה: Jewish mystical writings) and *Zohar* (זוהר: the chief work of the Kabbalistic movement). I don't want to press the connection too much, accept to say that they *all* represent—as does Christian apocalyptic—the writings of oppressed folk seeking refuge in a literary genre which envisions a soon-to-come answer from heaven, hidden in the writings of the ancient holy men.

The Evolution of a Revolution

Land of Israel ("Palestine," "The Holy Land"). They consisted of exegesis, amplifications, and discursive essays on the Pentateuch and Lamentations, Esther, Song of Songs and Ruth. Some of these compositions serve as word-for-word or verse-for-verse commentaries. Others present filigrees of scriptural verses so arranged as to make a point through dazzling bursts of prooftexts. What they have in common is the simple fact that they represent a totally new kind of book in their sort of Judaism....[221]

These Biblical explanations enabled some to find a measure of security at a time when security was in high demand but short supply. This was afforded the Jews by rabbinic Biblical exegetes who postulated that the upheaval of the day was predicted in Scripture. "Just as the Christians read stories of the Old Testament as types of the life of Christ, so the sages [of Israel] understood the tales of Genesis in a similarly typological manner."[222] Providing hidden meanings and messages, the Torah serviced esoteric interpreters who sought to prove that Jewish history was moving toward a definite providential end: the Messianic era.

Summary: On Christian and Jewish Histories

In ways similar to the church, and in other ways yet distinct from it, the synagogue was likewise bent on proving that God had predicted the events of the fourth and fifth centuries. St. Augustine's story begins in Genesis, where all the text's key players and events are reinterpreted to service St. Augustine's thesis—*the Christian triumph*. Though more soberminded than Eusebius,[223] he also subtly changes the

---

[221] Jacob Neusner, *Midrash in Context: Exegesis in Formative Judaism* (Philadelphia: Fortress Press, 1983), p. xi.
[222] Jacob Neusner, *Judaism and Christianity in the Age of Constantine*, p. 30.
[223] Here I'm referring to St. Augustine's understanding of earthly government.

The Evolution of a Revolution

natural (i.e., literal) meanings of Judaism's sacred text in order to service the church's need to have an authentic theological explication of the incredible turn of events in the forth and fifth centuries. After ascertaining how the above is apparent—through examining St. Augustine's treatment of Abraham, Isaac and Jacob, in his *City of God*[224] —we'll then note how Judaism's sages likewise used those very same biblical figures to service their particular needs and interests. We'll observe how that both Christian and Jewish communities are talking about the past, the present and the future and how both are using the same sourcebook—Genesis. Interestingly, we'll note how *both arrive at diametrically opposed conclusions.*

St. Augustine's Christological and Ecclesiological Treatment of Israel's Patriarchs
Introduction

St. Augustine has much to say about the *duo quaedam genera* (two kinds of cities): there those who live *secundum carnem* (according to the flesh) and *secundum se ipsum* (according to self), contrasted with those who live by Godly virtue—thus, the two commonwealths. Following his discussion on the origins of the two cities in Bks. XI-XIV, he then goes on to trace the respective cities' vicissitudes in Bks. XV-XVIII. Having reviewed the creation of angels (מַלְאָךְ or ἄγγελος), Adam (אָדָם or 'Αδάμ = "earth"[225]) and Eve (חַיָּה = "life"), he then goes on to discuss the race's development "from the time when the first pair began to produce offspring up to the time when mankind will cease to produce itself." (Bk. XV 1)—note how he's extremely interested in human history,[226] from start

---

[224] Being unable to work with the original Latin, I've chosen to work from Henry Bettenson's translation of St Augustine's classic *City of God* (London: Penguin Books, 1984).

[225] I don't know what source St. Augustine is using for his Hebrew names; I only know that he does have one. My source is Rabbi Alfred Kolatch's *The Complete Dictionary of English and Hebrew First Names* (Middle Village, NY: Jonathan-David Publishers, Inc., 1984).

The Evolution of a Revolution

to finish.[227]

Cain (קַיִן = "acquire" or "possess") was jealous of his brother Abel (הֶבֶל = "breath"), who was subsequently murdered as a result of Cain's "diabolical envy" (Bk. XV 5). Fratricide follows immediately after Adam and Eve's "original sin" and "fall."[228] Moving swiftly past Seth (שֵׁת = "garment" or "appointee," Bk. XV 15), Enos (אֱנוֹשׁ = "man," Bk. XV 17), Enoch (חֲנוֹךְ = "initiated," Bk. XV 17, 19), and Noah (נֹחַ = "rest, quiet, peace," Bk. XV 20ff), St. Augustine gets to Abraham (אַבְרָהָם = "father of the nation,"[229] Bk. XVI 12-15), Sarah (שָׂרָה = "noble" or "princess," Bk. XVI 19), Hagar (הָגָר = "emigration, forsaken, stranger," Bk. XVI 25), Ishmael (יִשְׁמָעֵאל = "God will hear," Bk. XVI 25), Isaac (יִצְחָק = "he will laugh," Bk. XVI 31, 36), and Jacob (יַעֲקֹב = "held by the heel," "protected" and/or "supplanted," Bk. XVI 37f). It's in Abraham and his progeny that "the oracles of God become more evident" (Bk. XVI 16); for God had כרת ברית (i.e., made/"cut" a covenant[230]) with the

---

[226] Cf., e.g. Bk.XXII, i.e., humans: (1) before the law, (2) under the law, (3) under grace, and (4) under peace.

[227] By "end" he's speaking of the consumation of this age. In this regard Dr. Richard Muller informs: *Consummatio saeculi:* consumation of the age (the Latin equivalent of συντέλεια τοῦ αἰῶνος, i.e., the end of the world) indicates the beginning of the next age or *saeculum*"; cf., *adventus Christi; dies novissimus; interitus mundi* (see Muller's *Dictionary of Latin and Greek Theological Terms* [Grand Rapids: Baker Book House, 1985], p. 81). St. Augustine has this termination of human history in view.

[228] St. Augustine notes how Rome began—as did the earthly city—with a record of fratricide: Romulus' murder of Remus. However, Romulus murdered Remus so that there would be but one city; whereas, Cain's murder of Abel marked the beginning of two cities (Bk. XV 5). This mindless slaughter is brought about by the "primal disobedience" of the first couple: Adam and Eve, through whom sin entered (Bk. XV 6). This inherited sickness—for St. Augustine a "defect in [man's] nature" which causes such human wreckage—is mended as one journey's through life practicing "Mutual forgiveness" and the "maintenance of peace"; says St. Augustine: "This is how the citizens of the City of God are restored to health while on pilgrimage on this earth, as they sigh for their Heavenly Country" (Bk. XV 6)."Loving concern for others" is to be valued over "domination" (Bk. XV 7). Mindful of this statement, I find it ironic that Christian domination over Judaism plays such a major role in his theology.

[229] Abram אַבְרָם with ה added (ה=God); now he represented the One God—יהוה.

[230] כרת ברית literally means to "cut a covenant." (Cf., XVI 24; Gen. 15:18f, when the covenant with Abraham was ratified.)

The Evolution of a Revolution

patriarch. What's in St. Augustine's Latin mind are allegories related to Christ and the Christian conquest.

Abraham: The Father of the Christian Nation

St. Augustine begins with the Abrahamic Covenant, recorded in Genesis 12: 1-3, wherein the patriarch is informed that he will be the father of a "great nation" (וְאֶעֶשְׂךָ לְגוֹי גָּדוֹל) that will be a great "blessing to all the families of the earth" (וְנִבְרְכוּ בְךָ כֹּל מִשְׁפְּחֹת הָאֲדָמָה; cf. Bk. XVI 16). Worthy of note is that for St. Augustine, *the great nation is the City of God, the Church—not the literal Jews.* He envisions Sarah as a type of the Virgin Mary. From Mary's womb came a miracle child, a son of Abraham, to bless the world. Sarah's miracle-born child serves as a prototype of Christ, through whom the promise to Abraham would be fulfilled (cf., Gal. 3:29, RSV: "if you are Christ's, then you are Abraham's offspring").

Gen. 17:7-8 reiterates the Divine promise, with an emphasis on the fact that the land of Canaan is to be given to Abraham's progeny (via Isaac) in perpetuity. The promise was that the covenant was to be established "throughout your generations" (לִבְרִית עוֹלָם), and that it's an "everlasting possession" (לַאֲחֻזַּת עוֹלָם). Not only was it reiterated to Abraham, but it was also recited to Isaac in Gen. 26:3-5: "To you [Isaac] and your descendants I will give all these lands and will confirm the oath I swore to your father Abraham." The explicit affirmation: "I will give all the land of Israel to you and your descendants" (כִּי־לְךָ וּלְזַרְעֲךָ אֶתֵּן אֶת־כָּל־הָאֲרָצֹת הָאֵל)[231] has been *reinterpreted* by St. Augustine:

> Yet the statement, 'I shall give it to you and to your seed after you', may puzzle some people, if they take 'for ever' (*usque in saeculum*) to mean

---

[231] In Gen. 28:3-4 it's Isaac, not Ishmael, who is given the Abrahamic blessing, and the right to the Land.—note the promise to Isaac: that "you may take possession of the land."

The Evolution of a Revolution

'for eternity.' If, on the other hand, they accept the word *saeculum* here in accordance with our confident belief that the beginning of the future era (*saeculum*) starts with the end of the present era, there will be nothing to puzzle them. For even though the Israelites have been expelled from Jerusalem, they still remain in other cities of the land of Canaan, and they will remain there to the end. And *the whole land, being inhabited by Christians, is itself the seed of Abraham*" (Italics mine; Bk. XVI 21).

Worthy of note is how *the Christian occupation of the land now fulfills the Abrahamic covenant.* Clearly, in St. Augustine's mind, Christianity now fulfills the scheme outlined in Genesis.[232] I believe that though St. Augustine was seeking to protect and defend the Scripture, *he weakened it by divesting it of its literal meanings,* opting instead to only envision prototypes of the Christian story.[233]

With the dawn of the *"ecclesia triumphans"* (i.e., the "Church Triumphant") there came a new way of looking at OT Scripture: the wonderful promises made to Abraham—the "father of *many* nations"—are now understood to be "fulfilled

---

[232] Again, in Bk. XVI 26, St. Augustine says: "If anyone is worried by the statement, 'And to your seed after you I shall give the land in which you are dwelling, all the land of Canaan for an *eternal possession*', and is puzzled about how this may be taken as being fulfilled..." know that the Greek for "eternal" (αἰώνιος from αἰών) corresponds to the Latin *saeculum* (i.e., of this age), and indicates that the covenant in Scripture lasts not in perpetuity, but till the "end of this [present] age"—i.e., as long as the earth. For St. Augustine, the promises regarding the glorious destiny of Abraham's progeny (cf., e.g. Gen. 12:1-3) are to be seen as fulfilled in God's new bride, the Church.

[233] By stating that the weak Jewish presence in Palestine confirms the promise to Abraham's literal descendants, he argues that the promise is literally true (though, of course the text calls for a triumphant Jewish state); but by reasoning that the Christian Church is both in the land and generally triumphant (both inside and outside of it), he reflects his allegorizing of the promise along with his reckoning that the Jews have been replaced in God's economy. I believe that he weakens the import of the Biblical promises because, by divesting Scripture of its actual literal meaning—i.e., God's love for the Jewish nation, etc.—one can make the text say whatever one wants it to say.

in Christ" and His *ecclesia universalis/catholica* (cf., Bk. XVI 28, and "through the Virgin" Bk. XVIII 1). The promise goes to "all nations according to faith" (Bk. XVI 29, cf. 21 the promise is to "spiritual rather than physical descendants"), in that "it is the sons of the promise [by faith] who are [now] counted as his [Abraham's] descendants" (Bk. XVI 32).

Isaac: As Both a Type of Christ and a Proof-Text for Gentile Christianity's Appropriation of the Abrahamic Covenant

St. Augustine knows that the Abrahamic covenant was reiterated to Isaac; but he is quick to cite Paul to offer a Christian explanation to the promise:

> The Apostle explains the force of 'Through Isaac your descendants will carry on your name' in this way: 'It does not mean that the sons of the flesh are the sons of God: *it is the sons of the promise who are counted as his descendants.*' Consequently, the sons of the promise are called in Isaac to be the descendants of Abraham, that is they are called by grace and gathered together in Christ (Italics mine; XVI 32).

Thinking himself to be following St. Paul's lead—and this should be open for discussion—St. Augustine divests the promise of its natural reading, and opts for a prophetic utterance which finds fulfillment in Christ. Not only do the biblical promises *all* find fulfillment in the church, Isaac's personal experience is even given a christological reading as well as an anti-Judaic interpretation.

Isaac's near-death experience on Moriah has serviced Christian kerygma for nealy two millennia. As the story goes, Isaac was about to have a dagger plunged into his breast by his father Abraham... but, in the knick of time Isaac was spared being sacrificed. Abraham was prevented from having to

The Evolution of a Revolution

perform the act, owing to God's having directed his attention toward a ram caught in the thicket which sufficed in place of Isaac—thus, God "provided" (יהוה יראה). This story provides St. Augustine with an interesting allegory: here he temporarily abandoned the classical Christian hermeneutical tradition (i.e., of simply envisioning a typology of Christ crucified) to deliberately misread a NT text in order to *take a shot at the Jews*: "Who then, was symbolized by that ram but Jesus, *crowned with Jewish thorns*[234] before he was offered as a sacrifice" (Italics mine; XVI 32). Certainly St. Augustine knows that Romans crowned Jesus with the thorns and *not* Jews.

In sum, through the allegorizing/typologizing of the promise made to Isaac, St. Augustine envisions that a triumphant Church has taken hold of the prophetic program. The Jews—those who have a genuine claim to being his progeny by nature—are now a rejected and condemned people, destined by God to live a life of painful servitude owing to their alleged wholesale rejection of Jesus Christ.

The Struggle Between Esau and Jacob: A Prophetic Mystery Predicting, Among Other Things, Christianity's Triumph Over the Jews.

In XVI 35, St. Augustine reflects upon the struggle between Jacob and Esau while yet unborn (cf. Gen 25:23). He mentioned that both had "original sin," while neither had, as of yet, any "personal sin." He has nothing more to say of their relationship[235] except that the prophecy "The elder shall

---

[234] In the Gospels Christ was crowned by the Roman soldiers, not the Jews (cf., e.g. Lk. 18:32 "For He will be delivered to the Gentiles and will be mocked and shamefully treated and spit upon."). Bettensen does mention that the crown of thorns was the work of Roman soldiers (p. 695, n. 150).

[235] Elsewhere he notes Bettensen, who cites: *Exp. Ep. ad Rom.; De Div. Quaest. ad Simpli.; Quaest. in Hept.* (n. 163, p. 698). As of yet, I haven't searched these references and so I must move cautiously here, knowing that I run an even higher-than-usual risk of making erronious assertions about things I really know nothing about. Besides, it's likely that I've already exhausted my readers' patience in that regard.

The Evolution of a Revolution

serve the younger" (וְרַב יַעֲבֹד צָעִיר) refers to, in St. Augustine's words, *"The older people of the Jews was destined to serve the younger people, the Christians"* (Italics mine; XVI 35). He notes that it could have some fulfillment in the Israelite conquest of the Idumaeans; however, he desires to accentuate the Christian triumph over Judaism by again stating, in closing: "And what can this meaning be except [an example of] a prophecy which is now being clearly fulfilled in the Jews and the Christians?" (*Ibid.*)

In XVI 37, commenting on the blessing that the elderly Isaac gave Jacob, he comes upon another allegorical message, one that's additionally alleged to be "pregnant with hidden meanings" (*Ibid.*) that are fulfilled in the Christian triumph. It's recorded in Gen. 27:27ff:

> [A]nd may God give you of the dew of heaven and of the richness of the soil, and abundance of corn and wine, and many nations serve you and princes do reverence to you. Become lord over your brother, and your father's sons will do reverence to you. Whoever curses you let him be cursed; and whoever blesses you, let him be blessed.

Herein we find a "hidden meaning conveying a profound truth" (*Ibid.*), one that may suffice to bring this section to a close. St. Augustine explains: the blessing is the proclamation of Christ among all the nations; the abundance of corn and wine is the eucharist; the princes are doing reverence to Christ, owing to the Christian triumph; Christ is the lord over His brother, since the Christians have dominion over the Jews (XVI 37). St. Augustine conveniently makes the Old Testament into one big allegory—of course, he wasn't alone in this approach to Christian Biblical hermeneutics.

The promises made to literal Israel have been allegorized and given ecclesiastical and Christological interpretations,

The Evolution of a Revolution

that have divested the text of its natural meaning. In what follows, we'll see how Judaism's sages did likewise allegorize Biblical texts to service their own needs and interests.

Genesis Rabbah: A Rabbinic Understanding of the Patriarchs as Typologies of Events Preceeding Judaism's Entrance into the Messianic Age

Introduction: The Mishnah and the Midrash

Having heard from St. Augustine, we'll now view the patriarchs refracted through the lenses of ancient rabbinic theology. We must hear from Judaism's sages without being interrupted by a considerable amount of comparative theological reflection. Mindful of this, the following will be concerned with the Jewish Midrash itself. *Genesis Rabbah*[236] (בראשית רבה, i.e. the Midrash on Genesis) will be contrasted with St. Augustine's work. After getting a clear view of what the Jewish sages were up to, we'll then return to St. Augustine and reflect upon the Christian and Jewish treatments of Scripture.

Abraham: An Exemplar for the Jewish Struggle in the Gentile World

In Genesis 12:1, Abraham is commanded by God to embark on a perilous journey into a strange new world. With little more than a prayer and a promise, he ventures forth, *by faith*, believing that he'll be triumphant at journey's end.

The midrashic sages inform that Abraham had to undergo a number of trials in advance of his receipt of God's blessing, [237] and that "his faith in the hour of trial won many converts."[238]

---

[236] Herein, I'll be using H. Freedman's translation (London, New York: Soncino Press, 1983).
[237] See Moshe Weissman,*The Midrash Says* (Union City: Benei Yakov Publications, 1980), passim.
[238] *The Midrash Rabbah*, trans. H. Freedman (London, New York: Soncino Press,

-145-

The Evolution of a Revolution

Commenting on the difficult trek, the rabbis opined: "The Holy One, blessed be He, first places the righteous in doubt and suspense, and then He reveals to them the meaning of the matter" (Lech Lecha, XXXIX 9). In *Genesis Rabbah*, Abraham serves as a prototype for a vanquished Jewish community in exile: like father, like sons; just as Abraham embarked on a strange and wonderful journey in the beginning, so must his offspring in the end of days.

לֶךְ לְךָ ("Lech Lecha," i.e., "go, go you/thou") says God to the noble patriarch, who was promised that he would become a blessing (12:2, וֶהְיֵה בְּרָכָה). How would he be a blessing to the world? It was understood by Judaism's sages to mean that Abraham made converts amongst the Gentiles to his monotheistic faith. The Midrash plays on the Hebrew for "blessing" (בְּרָכָה) being akin to another Hebrew word for "pool" (בְּרֵכָה) and says: "just as a pool purifies the unclean, so do thou bring near [to Me] those who are afar" (Lech Lecha, XXXIX 11).[239] Their case is built, in part, on the verse "Abraham took the souls he had made..." (וַיִּקַּח אַבְרָם וְאֶת־הַנֶּפֶשׁ אֲשֶׁר־עָשׂוּ בְחָרָן, Gen. 12:5). Explaining this, the Midrash says:

> [I]t refers to the proselytes [which they had made]. Then let it say, 'That they had converted'; why [then does the Scripture say] 'That they had made?' That is to teach you that he who brings a Gentile near [to God] is as though he created him... Said R. Hunia: "Abraham converted the men and

---

1983), n. 7, p. 316.

[239] Judaism's sages reasoned that Abraham baptized his converts—much like Christianity did and this accounts for the play on words with pool and blessing. This was not unique to the Midrash; in fact, debate over baptism, and legislation over the proper mode of performing it, appears in the Mishna (משנה, i.e., rabbinic writings of the late second century AD). Therein R. Joshua reasoned: "The mikveh [heb. for baptism] alone was needed and not circumcision." To the converse, R. Eliezer opined: "Circumcision alone was necessary and not the mikveh." With typical rabbinic diplomacy, it was eventually determined that both were necessary for converts. By way of contrast to Judaism's interpretation, we observe in *City of God* that St. Augustine understands the Abrahamic promise of world-blessing as speaking of conversion to Christianity (cf., Bk XVI).

The Evolution of a Revolution

Sarah the women" (Lech Lecha, XXXIX 14).

Furthermore, in addition to blessing the world by evangelizing it, Abraham's progeny likewise bless the Gentile world through their wisdom.[240]

> "And Jacob blessed Pharaoh" (Gen. XLVII, 7); moreover did not Joseph reveal his dreams to him, and did not Daniel reveal his dreams to Nebuchadnezzar?... R. Nehemiah said: The Holy One, blessed be He, said to Abraham: 'And in thee shall all the families of the earth be blessed'... it was meant in respect to counsel: when they [the Gentiles] get in trouble they ask our advice, and we give it to them" (Lech Lecha XXXIX, 12).

In sum, *Abraham serves as a type of ideal Israelite. Like Israel's exemplar, the Mishna's Hebrew nation is enroute toward a soon-to-be-realized "Promised Land."* Though beset by trials at present, redemption is just around the corner. Though hard-pressed, Israel can take heart; though vexed in spirit, Israel can/should/must have confidence in God. The Midrash understands that history is unfolding according to a pattern reflected in an allegorical interpretation of Genesis. Abraham's experience is employed by the midrashic sages to service their need to give hope to themselves as well as their discouraged and disoriented followers—people who'd been agonizing over both their defeat by the Church, and their own inability to see their aspirations realized.

Isaac and the Coming Messianic Kingdom

The story of Abraham's binding of Isaac (Gen. 22:1f) had long been viewed as a typology of Christ's sacrificial death. While Christians enjoyed using the text as a proof-text for

---

[240] It was best understood when explained with rabbinic authority, I might add

The Evolution of a Revolution

Christ's death, Judaism's sages found ways to use the story to evidence Judaism's triumph, when the Messiah will eventually come—an event in the future, from their vantage point.

Having heard from the Lord that Isaac must perish, Abraham leads Isaac and some family servants on an expedition to search for an ideal spot. Soon they approached a mount with a glory cloud enveloping it, which they interpreted as a signal that this must be the place for the sacrifice, Mt. Moriah (Vayera LVI 1). Abraham and Isaac are able to see the mountain "from afar" but the servants are unable (*Ibid.* 2):

> R. Isaac said: This place [i.e., Moriah—the site for the sacrifice and the eventual site of the Temple] will one day be alienated from its Owner [i.e., God]. Forever? [No], for it is stated, This is My restingplace for ever; here will I dwell for I have desired it; (Ps CXXXII, 14)—when he comes of whom it is written, Lowly, and riding on an ass (Zech. I, 9) (Ibid.).

The point here is that the Temple mount is inaccessible to the Owner—God; for now the people can only see "afar off." One day, however, He and His people will have access to the Temple, when the Messiah comes, of whom it says He will come on an ass.[241]

In saying to the servants "we will come back," the Midrash understands that Abraham knew that both he and Isaac would return. The rabbis have a special way of employing the saying "We will worship and return to you" (וְנִשְׁתַּחֲוֶה וְנָשׁוּבָה אֲלֵיכֶם, in Gen. 25:10); they see that *return follows worship*. Note the following rabbinic gloss on the text in Genesis:

> The exiles will return only as a reward for

---

[241] By way of contradistinction we note how St. Augustine opined that the Christian conquest of the Holy Land was predicted in various Abrahamic typologies. Here, Judaism's sages see Christianity's displacement from Palestine in Abrahamic passages.

The Evolution of a Revolution

> worshipping: And it shall come to pass in that day, that a great horn shall be blown; and they shall come that were lost... and they shall worship the Lord in the holy mountain at Jerusalem (Isa. XXVII, 12). The Temple was built only as a reward for worshipping... The dead will come to life again only as a reward for worshipping... (Vayera LVI 2).

If Israel would only worship God correctly—i.e., according to the dictates of the rabbis—the long-awaited deliverance would come (i.e., redemption from Christian oppression,[242] resurrection, etc.).

Commenting on Abraham's building the altar and then binding Isaac (Gen. 22:9), the sages say:

> R. Hanina b. Isaac said: Even as Abraham bound his son Isaac below, so the Holy One, blessed be He, bound the princes of the heathens above. Yet they did not remain [thus bound]. For when Israel alienated themselves [from God, the oppressive heavenly hosts were unleashed against the Jews.] (Vayera, LVI 5).

Herein, the Christian conquest is seen as a punishment for not worshipping God correctly.

With regard to the ram in the thicket, which served as a sacrifice and thus redeemed Isaac from the altar, the rabbis envision a prediction of Judaism's punishment for sin as well as her eventual redemption:

> What does *ahar*[243] [ram] mean? Said R. Judan:

---

[242] The initial conquest and oppression of the Jews in the C. E. came at the hands of the Romans long before Christianity became a serious player on the religio-political scene (Dr. William Babcock). Nevertheless, at the penning of the Midrash it was "Christian" Rome which sought to denigrate the Jews much more than the various civil administrations.

The Evolution of a Revolution

> After all that happened [i.e., after all God did for Israel in bringing the nation out of Egypt, etc.] Israel still fell into the clutches of sin and [in consequence] became the victim of persecution; yet they will be ultimately redeemed by the ram's horn, as it says *And the Lord will blow the horn, etc.* (Zech. IX, 14). R. Judah b. R. Simon interpreted: At the end of all generations Israel will fall into the clutches of sin and be the victim of persecution; yet eventually they will be redeemed by the ram's horn.... (Vayera, LVI 9).

Then, the text is worked into a divinely ordained narrative:

> R. Abba b. R. Pappi and R. Joshua of Siknin in R. Levi's name said: Because the Patriarch Abraham saw the ram extricate himself from one thicket and go and become entangled in another, the Holy One, blessed be He, said to him: So will thy children be entangled in countries, changing from Babylonia to Media, from Media to Greece, and from Greece to Edom [Rome]; yet they will eventually be redeemed by the ram's horn, as it is written, *And the Lord God will blow the horn... and the Lord of hosts will defend them...* (Vayera, LVI 9).

There is much to say about how the texts are employed to tell of the domination and subsequent release in the Messianic era. Let's now consider how Jacob and Esau texts are employed.

The Struggle Between Esau and Jacob: A Typology Foreshadowing the Conflict Between Displaced Judaism and Triumphant Roman Christianity

Rebekah, Jacob's beloved wife, was informed: "Two nations are in thy womb" (שְׁנֵי גיִֹים בְּבִטְנֵךְ, Gen. 25:23) and that "There are two rulers of nations in thy womb, Hadrian of the Gentiles and

---

[243] איל in *Biblia Hebraic Stuttgartensia,* which reproduces the Leningrad Codex B19a (L).

The Evolution of a Revolution

Solomon of Israel" (Toledoth LXIII 7). Hadrian harks back to a Roman emperor and Solomon to a Jewish religious monarch. In regard to the allegorical meaning and destiny of each great[244] child, R. Helbo, says in the name of the School of R. Shila: "[F]rom thee shall arise Jews and Arameans [Romans]" (*Ibid.*). It's evident in the Midrash that *Esau was understood by the Jews to be a type depicting Roman rule.*[245]

We're told that Esau (Rome) is offensive to God—which should be understood by moderns to mean that Rome was offensive to the vanquished ancient Israelites. For example, in regard to the Biblical statement that "Esau came forth ruddy," the Midrash asked and answered: Question: "Why did Esau issue first? [Answer:] So that he might issue and all the offensive matter with him" (Toledoth, LXIII 8)—i.e., all the defilement. Not even trying to mask their contempt for imperial and religious Rome, the rabbis refer to Esau as a swine who is given the name Diocletian—a Roman emperor! (*Ibid.*)

With a new understanding of Genesis, the sages alleged that Moses had picked up on the imagery that swine depict religious/imperial Rome's cunning and perfidy.[246] The sages asked:

> Why does he [Moses] compare it [the Romans] to a swine? For this reason: when the swine is lying down it puts out its hoofs, as if to say, 'I am clean';

---

[244] The sacred text notes that they "jostled within her" (וַיִּתְרֹצֲצוּ הַבָּנִים בְּקִרְבָּהּ); to this the Midrash adds that these were "proud nations" in that גיים = "nations" and גאים = "proud ones."

[245] The Scripture went on to say "the elder shall serve the younger," and this prompts the following, in the Midrash: "R. Huna commented: If he [Jacob] is deserving, he [Esau] shall serve him; if not he [Esau] shall enslave him" (Toledoth LXIII 7). The point is that if Israel doesn't obey God's law, then Israel will be ruled by Esau—i.e. Rome (by association now, Christian Rome). This serves as a locus for an ancient Jewish understanding: the rise of the Roman religious state and the continual rapid dismembering of the Jewish community (thus the "enslavement" spoken of) is indicative of God's temporary judgment on Israel.

[246] See *The Midrash Rabbah*, Vol. 2, p. 581, n. 2.

The Evolution of a Revolution

so does this wicked State rob and oppress, yet pretend to be executing justice" (Toledoth, LXV 1).

According to the Pentateuch, animals with split hoofs were kosher—i.e., clean, fit for consumption. The pig is a defiled creature with a split hoof; thus, say the sages, this detestable beast attempts to pass itself off as clean, while it isn't. Given Church's claim to having become the new Jews, Judaism responds informing that this dogmatic assertion as tantamount to "swine putting forth their split hooves"—i.e., an attempt of defiled creatures to deceive others into thinking that they are kosher.[247] Contrary to the Christian theologians, the Israelites are the genuine people of the book—not the Romans, with their corrupted misappropriation of Judaism's sacred Scripture. Commenting on the naming of the boy Esau, the sages said: "'Ye have given a name to your swine [Esau]; then I too will name my firstborn,' as it says, 'Thus says the Lord: Israel is my son, My firstborn (Ex. IV, 22)'" (Ibid.). The Midrash knows, as does the reader of Genesis, that Esau (the swine) will not forever prevail. This section (i.e. LXIII) closes with: "make a reminder that the birthright belongs to Jacob" (Toledoth, LXIII 14).

In sum, though chosen by God, Jacob must, for a season, endure the lawless Esau.[248] Though the mighty Esau came first—just as the Roman occupation has, in advance of the Messianic era[249]—it's clear that nevertheless Jacob (i.e.,

---

[247] In evidence of their corruption, note how vexation over the Roman triumph resulted in the following lamentation: "Israel cried out before God: 'Sovereign of the Universe! Is it not enough that we have been subject to the seventy nations [i.e., the peoples of the world], but must we be subject to this one too [i.e., Esau—Rome], who is immorally abused, *like women*" (Italics mine; Toledoth, LXIII 10). Jews believed that Romans often practiced sodomy. Since they used men like women, some of their men became like women; in fact, one day they'll all be like women—says the Midrash: "And the heart of the mighty men of Edom at that day shall be as the heart of the woman in her pangs (Jer. XLIX, 22)" (Ibid.).

[248] In Toledoth, LXIII 12 Esau is guilty of defiling a maiden, commiting murder and theft.

[249] A view that makes the horrid Roman oppression hopeful in a strange way.

The Evolution of a Revolution

Israel) was/is God's favorite and that he will finally prevail.

> A [Roman] prefect asked a member of the family of Salu: 'Who will enjoy power after us? [i.e., after Rome]' [In reply] he [the Jew] brought a blank piece of paper, took a quill and wrote upon it, 'And after that came forth his brother [Jacob], and his hand had hold on Esau's heel.' Upon this the comment was made: 'See how ancient words become new in the mouth of a Sage!' (Toledoth, LXIII 9).

The point of the pericope in view is simple: In the Esau-Jacob allegory, Judaism will triumph over Christian Rome. This simple overarching theme surfaces in each of the patriarchal stories, and evidences how the biblical text was employed to service Judaism's crisis, just as it was used by St. Augustine to demonstrate Christianity's conquest.

Judaism and Christianity both needed a theological explication of world events. Both believed that God was moving history along according to His preordained plan; so it became necessary to show exactly what that plan was. Both groups went to the protological texts (i.e., Genesis) to show how their view of history's movement in the end was predicted in the beginning. Having juxtaposed both the Christian and Jewish interpretations, and having seen how the respective exegetes operate in similiar fashion, we're now ready to make some evaluations and bring this to a close.

Summary

Having read all the above, I ask: Exactly *what* was St. Augustine, the 5th century Christian historiographer, doing with Judaism's phylogenetic history, and *why* was he doing it?; also, What were the midrashic sages doing, and why?

The Jews were a beaten people and they searched the Scriptures to find ways to help them deal with their pain. The

The Evolution of a Revolution

Latin churchmen however, for the most part, were intoxicated by their triumph in the empire. They, searched those same scriptures to service their own needs—needs we'll now consider.

What Needs St. Augustine was Servicing
Need for a Contemporary Theological Exposition

St. Augustine was interested in providing a systematic retelling of the Bible's story, with his own thesis in view—i.e., the Christian triumph in the Roman empire. To do so successfully: (1) Judaism had to be slain on the exegetical altar—so it was; (2) Christianity had to be found within the Old Testament text—so it was; (3) Rome's embrace of Christianity had to be found as well—so it was; (4) the world-to-come (i.e., afterlife) would likewise need to be ascertained within the Old Testament texts—so it was; (5) the thesis would need to be presented in a manner that would speak to the Greco-Roman mind (this would require employing classical Greek and Roman literature as well)—and so it was.

The Method Employed to Service the Need

St. Augustine employed an allegorical approach to Biblical exegesis—an approach *not* uncommon amongst Jews—believing that he was able to ascertain the text's hidden/typological meanings.[250] His allegorical methodology allowed him—as it did/does others—to make his own spiritual concoctions, unbridled by the conventions of common sense. This is evidenced in how he divests the Genesis account of the literal meaning of the words in order to make "spiritual" applications for a "grafted in" (Rom. 11:17-24) Christian community[251]—he does this with the New Testament as well (e.g., the millennial kingdom; cf. Rev. 20:1-3, Bk. XX, passim). St. Augustine had trouble with the Bible's literal readings. Why? He was

---

[250] It should be noted that he was following a well established Christian hermeneutical tradition in this regard.
[251] The Jews got "shafted" when the Gentiles got "grafted."

The Evolution of a Revolution

discouraged over the prospect of any earthly "Christian" paradise—called "over-realized eschatology," today; for this reason, St. Augustine made a break with millennialism—even though it was a major component in early orthodox theology[252]—and opted to simply spiritualize New Testament texts that required an earthly fulfillment.[253]

If one believed in a literal interpretation of the Bible one may perhaps have been forced to acknowledge God's love for the literal/physical Jews—and see hope for the restoration of their kingdom.[254] St. Augustine didn't even want to envision a literal Christian millennial kingdom, preferring a purely spiritual commonwealth instead. Irenaeus, on the other hand, saw a resplendent earthly Christian Jerusalem, as did Tertullian.[255] In fact, it was Gaius—a third century presbyter who opposed the book of Revelation on the ground that he believed it to be written by Cerinthus (a Gnostic)[256]—who was the first to interpret the thousand year reign symbolically.[257]

---

[252] Of course, one could argue that prior to the councils and creeds, what we had was a heterodoxical situation which would allow for more diversity.

[253] I make this point in fairness to St. Augustine. *He wrote off notions of a literal Christian kingdom, as well as a future for a Jewish one.* This then leads me to believe that his approach was other-worldly—i.e., it's not that he was specifically against the Jews, rather he was against a belief in a future for God's accomplishments on this earth (except for assorted Christian gains for souls), opting instead to look for the coming spiritual commonwealth in the eschaton.

[254] Frankly, however, I must admit that this wasn't very likely back then. I'm happy to report though that this is a major characteristic in some evangelical theologies today (e.g., Dallas Theological Seminary, Moody Bible Institute, etc.). *Today's literal premillennialists argue that there will be a thousand year kingdom with national Israel restored, in accordance with the literal reading of the Bible.* (cf., Charles Ryrie, *What You Should Know About Inerrancy* [Chicago: Moody Press, 1981], p. 16; Paul Enns, *The Moody Handbook of Theology* [Chicago: Moody Press, 1989], p. 52; and Paul L. Tan, *The Interpretation of Prophecy* [Rockville, MD: Assurance Publishers,, 1974], passim).

[255] *Early Christian Doctrines*, 467-469; from *Dominion Theology: Blessing or Curse* (Portland: Multnomah Press, 1988), p. 203.

[256] Elizabeth Livingston, *The Concise Oxford Dictionary of the Christian Church* (Oxford: Oxford University Press, 1977), p. 99 and p. 204. See F. L. Cross' edition of the *Oxford Dictionary*, p. 535, used in *Dominion Theology: Blessing or Curse*, p. 204.

[257] *Dominion Theology: Blessing or Curse*, p. 204.

The Evolution of a Revolution

This view was embraced by Clement of Alexandria, Origen, St. Augustine[258] as well as many modern-day Christians.[259]

Dr. J. N. D. Kelly is quite helpful in explaining St. Augustine's situation further:

> The clash with Judaism and paganism made it imperative to set out the bases of the revealed dogmas more throughly. [Furthermore,] The Gnostic tendancy to dissolve eschatology into the myth of the soul's upward ascent and return to God [likewise] had to be resisted....[260]

Dr. Kelly opines that it was necessary for the church to set out their own dogmas *distinct* from Judaism[261]—and Gnosticism; this, of course, required a *reinterpretation of the Jewish Scriptures, with a reapplication to Christianity.*[262]

---

[258] Cf, e.g., Bk. XX, passim.

[259] It's for this reason that many Bible-believing churchmen reject the modern assertion—held by some—that present-day Israel is a fulfillment of Bible prophecy. Says the Rev'd Dr. A.C. Forest: "The Christian press and pulpit need to take more seriously than others the World Council of Churches appeal... Not only have many editors and preachers sold their credibility for free trips to the Holy Land, they have distorted the Scriptures and misled their people. The World Council of Churches added an injunction: 'The subject of Biblical interpretation must be studied in order to avoid the misuse of the Bible in support of partisan political views [i.e., Israel as a Jewish homeland]...' In May 1970, a Beirut conference of world Christians on Palestine put it more bluntly: 'We reject the manipulation of Biblical texts for the purpose of political power'" (A. C. Forrest, *The UnHoly Land* [Toronto: McClelland & Stewart Limited, 1972], p. 166).

[260] Italics mine; J. N. D. Kelly, *Early Christian Doctrines* (San Francisco: Harper & Row, 1978), p. 465; from H. Wayne House and Thomas Ice, *Dominion Theology: Blessing or Curse?*, pp. 202-203.

[261] A Jewish belief in a literal 1,000 year kingdom-period is evidenced in *The Book of Enoch* 1:3b-9; 5:7; 10:17-22; 11:1-2; *The Ezra Apocalypse* 5:1; 12: 13; 13: 29-38; *The Apocalypse of Baruch* 70: 2-10; 73:1-7; 29:5-8.

[262] St. Jerome wrote a number of books entitled *Against the Jews*. The reason was that he didn't want Christians to fraternize with Jews. This is worth bringing up here as a testimony of how the Church felt it necessary to forge an identity distinct from Judaism. This would mean reinterpreting the Jews' sacred texts, something that St. Augustine does so well and so often.

The Evolution of a Revolution

The Need for a Credible Theological and Historiographical Exposition

A literal reading of Genesis simply didn't make sense to a number of ancient Christians, for whom the OT's "Chosen People" (physical Jews) were hounded undesireables, perceived as creatures descended from a condemned and rejected race. For the Latin Christians, if Scripture was to be credible, it would have to be because of its spiritual meanings hidden behind its literal words.

B. The Christian Re-Interpretation of Judaism's Sacred Space

Introduction

In what follows we will examine other aspects of the Latin Christian world of the fourth and early fifth centuries. We will enter the world of another noteworthy monastic, Paulinus of Nola, a good friend of St. Augustine, who gives us another window into ancient Christian life and literature.

Paulinus was an architect, a builder and poet, etc. What will we learn from this talented monk? We will discover how—as was the case with St. Augustine—Christian theologians reinterpreted Jewish literature, faith and practice to service the Christian church.

About Paulinus: Brief History

St. Paulinus (Pontius Meropius) of Nola was born into a privileged Christian family around 353A.D. in Bordeaux. Paulinus was first educated under Ausonius.[263] Following Ausonius' departure from Bordeaux, Paulinus went on to get a thorough education in law and rhetoric,[264] preparing for a

---

[263] In addition to having some influence on Paulinus, Ausonius was tutor to Gratianus, a consul and even the Court poet. See Goldschmidt, Rudolf Carel, *Paulinus' Churches at Nola: Texts, Translations and Commentary* (Amsterdam: N.V. Noord-Hollandsche Uitgevers Maatschappi, 1940), p. 3.

[264] Goldschmidt says of his abilities: "He knew the classic poets very well, their

The Evolution of a Revolution

future which seemed quite promising. He is said to have received a consulship in 378, after which he was quickly advanced by Gratianus to several other offices of importance.[265] However, with Gratianus' fall in 383, both Ausonius and Paulinus lost their protector. Paulinus—a man who seemingly had everything going for him—retreated to Spain where he married the wealthy and pious Therasia.

The repose of newlywed bliss was short lived. The young couple settled in Catalonia and gave birth to a son named Celsus. Sadly, however, the child died at the tender age of eight days. About this time Paulinus' brother was murdered for political reasons. In addition to his being traumatized by the loss of his son and brother, the affairs of his own estate were jeopardized by the political intrigue surrounding his brother's assassination. Once again, Paulinus' promising future was threatened just as it was following Gratianus' fall. Paulinus and Therasia found themselves pressed amidst the turbulence of trying times: the death of young Celsus and the precariousness of political life, with the savagery of political intrigue, all served to shake their foundations, causing the young couple to ask questions about life's meaning and purpose.

Exigencies drove the young couple to their knees. Through the exhortation of St. Ambrose, they eventually divested themselves of most of their worldly goods—apparently they were quite well endowed—and together they embarked on a spiritual quest. Their enthusiasm for their journey won them the admiration of a number of contemporary Christian noteworthies (e.g., St. Ambrose, St. Augustine and St. Jerome), and evoked the indignation of some others (e.g., Ausonius and even Pope Siricius[266]).

---

technique and their expressions are entirely at his disposal. He consequently writes in cultivated Latin and seldom infringes upon metrical rules." (Ibid., p. 6)

[265] *Cyclopedia of Biblical, Theological and Ecclesiastical Literature*, Vol. VII., ed. John McClintock and James Strong (Grand Rapids: Baker Books, 1981), p. 837. Both this and Goldschmidt's work (see above) serve as sources for my biographical information on Paulinus.

The Evolution of a Revolution

Eventually, Paulinus and Therasia—finally now ascetics bound together by a purely spiritual non-carnal alliance (i.e., they *didn't* have sexual relations)—made their way to Nola (in 394), where Paulinus had once owned some property.[267] As was typical of monastics, Paulinus, Therasia and some of their followers took up residence over a martyr's (better "Confessor's") tomb: Felix—a local priest, known for exorcisms and for having both performed and received miracles.[268] So enamored was Paulinus of his confessor Felix, that he constructed an edifice in his honor—a facility that will be investigated in what follows. By studying Paulinus'e art and architecture we can get a window into the 4th century Christian world where he shined as a luminary. As we examine his buildings and poetry, we'll discover how, unknown to Paulinus, his religious churches housed an amalgam of Jewish and Christian themes and texts, welded together with assorted imperial Greco-Roman motifs.

Methodological Approach: How We Will Study the Nolan Complex

Sadly, the spiritual citadel dedicated to Felix, which once proudly marked the religious landscape of ancient Latin

---

[266] Goldschmidt conjectures that perhaps he was threatened owing to Paulinus' popularity.

[267] Other family holdings which he'd relinquished were in Aquitania, Gallia Narbonensis, Fundi at Latium and possibly in Spain too. (Goldschmidt, *Paulinus' Churches at Nola*, p. 3)

[268] In *Natalicium* V, C. 16, 299vv, Paulinus retells the story how Felix was spared during the Decian persecution. Goldschmidt opines that Felix's story was likely derived from David's miracle, recounted in Targum Ps. 7—the Aramaic translation of the psalm—wherein David rejoices over his miraculous deliverance from Saul when God reached down from heaven and saved him (ישלח משמים ויושיעני). He is aware that there are similar stories in other cultures; however, he says: "All European and oriental versions may have derived from the Jewish legend"—i.e., thus from the Targum mentioned above. (Goldschmidt, *Paulinus' Churches at Nola*, p. 8). He then goes on to inform that Felix was a Syrian. That being the case, Felix may have had knowledge of Jewish oriental mysticism which may then have filtered down to Paulinus (*Cyclopaedia of Biblical, Theological and Ecclesiastical Knowledge*, Vol. III, p. 523).

The Evolution of a Revolution

Christianity, has long since fallen—as has the memory of Felix for that matter. All that remains of the structure are the some of the foundations which protrude from the earth at Cimitile. Owing to the fact that the buildings, paintings and mosaics are lost to us, it behooves me to address the question of *how* I intend to resurrect the Nolan complex in order to study it.

Herein I intend to first examine, as best as I can, what there is of the the archeological remains of the Nolan basilicas (the basic floorplan etc.), as well as some of Paulinus' literary works; additionally, I will compare the imagery in the literary texts to some of the other art works from the period that are extant. From the above, a reasonable picture will appear—I believe.

Basilicas in General and the Site at Cimitile in Particular
About Basilicas in General
Greco-Roman Prototypes (archetype)

Webster defined a basilica as "an oblong building ending in a semicircular apse, used in ancient Rome especially for a court of justice and place of public assembly."[269] The appellation "basilica" is a Latin word derived from a Greek source. βασιλεία (basileia) is a Greek word denoting royal power, dominion, etc., which is derived from βασιλεύς (basileus) meaning simply "king."[270] Put simply, prior to their use for religious purposes, basilicas were Roman buildings housing some sort of official authoritative decision making aparatus; they were religious palaces—said to have been vested with special sacral authority much like the Old Testament's special house of worship.[271]

---

[269] *Webster's Seventh New Collegiate Dictionary* (Springfiled, Mass.: G. & C. Merriam Company, 1969), p. 72.

[270] Vines, *Expository Dictionary of New Testament Words* (McClean, Va.: McDonald Publishing), pp. 633-634. Let me note here that I'm only able to work with original languages with the help of basic language tools (see below).

The Evolution of a Revolution

Hebrew Prototype (archetype)
The Old Testament's Tabernacle served as a prototype for Christian basilicas; for this reason, I think it would be helpful if we spent a few moments and acquanited ourselves with it.

In Old Testament Hebrew, God's kingship was represented by מלוכה or ממלכה[272]; like βασιλεία, this word is also derived from a word for king: מלך (meleck).[273] Israel's King (God) dwelled at first, in the אהל מועד ("Tent of Meeting"), which was simply called the משכן ("Dwelling")—i.e., His portable basilica constructed during Israel's wanderings following the nation's rescue from Egyptian bondage. Once in the "Promised Land," however, God's living quarters[274] were upgraded to genuine basilica status. Known as the היכל ("palace"), Solomon's Temple became a national monument; sadly, however, it was destroyed by the Babylonians in 586 B.C.E. Following the Persian conquest of Babylonia, Cyrus decreed that the Judeans could return and rebuild their sancturay (Ezra 1:2-3). Their rebuilt Sanctuary was eventually desecrated by Antiochus IV, rededicated following the Maccabean revolt, and restored by Herod.[275] Inscribed on some of the Herodian columns was the following יכין ה כסא דוד ומלכותו לורעו עד עולם, meaning: "May the Lord establish the throne of David and His kingdom for His seed forever!" Sadly for the Jews, the hopes reflected in this inscription were not to be realized: the Temple was destroyed.

---

[271] See J. Seif and Z. Levitt, *The House That God Built: The Tabernacle in the Wilderness* (Dallas: Zola Levitt Ministries, 1989).

[272] Also מלכות השמים (="Kingdom of Heaven"); see the *The Complete Hebrew-English Dictionary*, ed. R. Alcalay (Massada/Yedioth Ahronoth: Chemed Books, 1990), p. 2042.

[273] *Theological Wordbook of the Old Testament,* Vol. 1,, ed. R. Laird Harris (Chicago: Moody Press, 1980), p. 507.

[274] Sometimes it was known simply as בית, meaning "house"—by implication, God's house.

[275] For a brief treatment of the history of the Temple, written in popular prose, see Seif and Levitt, *The House That God Built* (Dallas: Zola Levitt Ministries, 1989), pp. 54-60.

The Evolution of a Revolution

Christian Basilicas Contain an Amalgam of Old Testament and Greco-Roman Motifs

Paulinus made his entrance onto the stage of the human drama at a time when the glory of Israel's first and second Temples had long since faded. Owing to the recent Christian triumph in the empire, it was perceived by many that the Church had replaced and/or displaced Israel in God's economy, in the process becoming the new and improved "Chosen People" of God. The Christian reinterpretation of Judaism's תורה (Scripture) with an understanding that the Christian ἐκκλησία or συνάγωγη (Church) had become the new ישראל (Israel) had been around for quite a few years[276]; but Christianity's sublation of Judaism's "Holy House" (בית המקדש), as well as the re-designation of Israel's "Promised Land" as the Christian "Holy Land," were innovative characteristics of the fourth century[277]—a century which began with Christians' being persecuted by the state,[278] and ended with them gaining more and more control of it.

And so, constructed in an age when the "Church Triumphant" had seized hold of the modern world, the Nolan basilicas—like all basilicas—reflected this amazing victory. For many years prior, the Church had told its story by *humbly* depicting Biblical figures, understood to be representative innate typologies of Jesus Christ (e.g. Abraham's offering up Isaac, etc.). What was unique to the fourth century was the way in which various Christian art works were embellished by the appropriation of symbols of, and techniques from, *imperial*

---

[276] Cf. e.g., Justin Martyr's *Dialogue With Trypho*, passim.

[277] See Robert Markus, "Holy Places and Holy People," in *The End of Ancient Christianity* (Cambridge: Cambridge University Press, 1990), pp. 139-155.

[278] From 303-311, emperor Diocletian Galerius launched what was the worst of the ten waves of persecution against the Church. Churches and Bibles were destroyed; all civil rights were suspended; sacrifice to gods was mandatory. See Robert Walton's *Chronological and Background Charts of Church History* (Grand Rapids: Zondervan/Academie Books, 1986), p. 10.

The Evolution of a Revolution

art—used now to tell the story of Christianity's new-found imperial favor and subsequent strength.

About the Ruins of Paulinus' Basilicas at Cimitile in Particular

Sadly, not much remains of Paulinus' Nolan complex today. The site at Cimitile had been explored by Ambrosius Leone in 1594 and Gianstefano Remondini in 1747. In 1890, Baldoria and others frequently complained of the shrine's neglect. Eventually, in 1933, new excavations were begun, and a report on the findings followed in 1939. Gino Chierici's published report, in *Atti del IV Congresso Nazionale di Studi Romani*, was disappointing to Goldschmidt, who lamented that the ground plan wasn't especially clear. One of the only salient features, according to Dr. Goldschmidt, was Chierici's ability to "prove a [lack of a] relation[ship] between the Nolan sanctuary and the Church of the Holy Sepulchre"[279]—*something that I will hotly contest.*

Reconstructing the Nolan Basilicas Through Extant Literary Sources

Viewing the Nolan Basilica and Church of the Holy Sepulchre Against the Backdrop of the Jerusalem Temple

Paulinus, through his writings, describes more of the particulars of the Nolan complex. Following is a close examination of the literature. Paulinus' statements are indicated by quotation marks.

Examining the ceremonial functions at the Nolan complex we note the following. (1) Paulinus' basilica, like the Old Testament's, comes replete with a "holy altar" (Epistula 32

---

[279] Goldschmidt argues, contrary to Bertaux and Byvanck, that it's useless to try and prove a relation between the Nolan sanctuary and the Church of the Holy Sepulchure, on the basis of the slim archeological remains. (Goldschmidt, *Paulinus' Churches at Nola*, p. 20) While this may be true, I'm hoping to demonstrate possible connections in other ways.

The Evolution of a Revolution

§11), upon which "Holy libations" are poured (Carmen 27, 405). This is similar to the מובח (altar) in Ex. 27:1f. (2) The Nolan holy altar is associated with it's Christianized "Holy of Holies" (cf. Ex. 26: 34, קדש הקדשים, i.e. "most holy place") as evidenced by the following inscription: "Peace be with all ye who enter the Holy of Holies of Christ" (Epistula 32 §12). (3) Just who enters the Christian temple's inner sanctums? A Christian priesthood—a concept borrowed from Judaism's כהנים—enters: "Enter there, priest, singing psalms and hymns" (Carmen 27, 500); this is akin to the Levitical priesthood who were "called out" to serve the sanctuary in the Old Testament. (4) The bishop "consecrates the venerable Holy of Holies by associating the holy sacraments with the purifying font" (Carmen 28, 185-190); much like Judaism's temple cult, the Nolan basilica comes with a ritual font for cleansings, even likened to waters in the Temple of Solomon (Epistula 32 §15; Carmen 27, 475-480).[280] (5) Just as Judaism's "Holy Place" was enclosed within a courtyard, thus set apart from the Israelite community, so Paulinus says: "the holy house should not stand open to profane eyes and that a courtyard, open to the air, should protect the holy of holies" (Carmen 27, 490). (6) Lastly, just as Solomon's temple was filled with the "Glory cloud" (cf. 2 Chron. 5:13-14), so too, Paulinus likewise believes that: "Christ will benevolently descend to wrap the people and the temple in a holy cloud" (Carmen 27, 505-510; cf., Ex. 40: 33-34).[281]

Obviously, Paulinus *re*-employs biblical language and imagery—employed in the Scripture to cast light on the goings on within Judaism's sacred Temple—to describe the Nolan basilicas.

---

[280] Latin *Cantharus*. (Goldschmidt, *Paulinus' Churches at Nola*, pp. 114-115)

[281] In his commentary on Carmen 27, 510, Goldschmidt observed that Paulinus' statement about God's descending in a cloud to His Sacarium, is akin to that in Epistula 31 §6, 273, 26, used to describe the Church of the Holy Sepulchre in Jerusalem. (Goldschmidt, *Paulinus' Churches at Nola*, p. 152)

The Evolution of a Revolution

Comparing the Nolan Complex With Egeria's Diary

Down from antiquity has come another sterling example of the Christian sublation of Judaism's Temple and sacrifical system. In *Egeria: Diary of a Pilgrimage*[282] a woman, Egeria, gave an account of her three year pilgrimage to Jerusalem around the year 417A.D. Of special note is the way she described the worship at the Church of the Holy Sepulchre. (1) In chapter 24 Egeria spoke of a "light that burns perpetually" (cf., the מנרה), akin to the light in Ex. 25: 31-40; 27:20-21); (2) in 27 she referred to the "offering of the sacrifice" which is called the "divine service," an obvious reference to the celebration of the eucharist, a liturgical rite with theological root in Judaism's sacrificial cult (Israel's יום כפר, i.e., the "Day of Atonement"; see Lev. 16:1-34, esp. 32-34; Ex. 29:38-42), specifically in Judaism's passover celebration[283]; (3) in 30 she observes how "Holy Week," i.e., Passion Week, is referred to there as the "Great Week," the term used at Judaism's Feast of Tabernacles (סכות, cf., Lev. 23: 33-44; Jn. 7:37[284]); (4) in 48, she informs that the day when the "Martyrium," i.e., the holy church on Golgotha, was dedicated to God, is called by the name "Feast of Dedications" and is observed for eight days, much like Channukah (חנוכה)—i.e., the dedicatory feast commemorating the Maccabean purge of Antiochus Epiphanes' desecration of the Jerusalem Temple in 168 B.C.E.[285]).

With regard to the Church of the Holy Sepulchre, Dr. Robert Milburn, a Church historian at Oxford, observed:

> The majestic combination of holy places on Golgotha so impressed the [Christian] historians that they likened

---

[282] *Egeria: Diary of a Pilgrimage*, trans. George E. Gingras, in *Ancient Christian Writers* Vol. 38, ed. Johannes Quasten, Walter J. Burghardt and Thomas Comerford Lawler (New York: Newman Press, 1970).

[283] See Seif, *Origin of the Christian Faith* (Dallas: JSM and CFNI, 1992), pp. 31-45.

[284] On the eighth day of Tabernacles one single bullock was offered for Israel's sins (פר יחידי למהכנגד אומה יחידה); of the eighth day, the rabbis say: it is a feast by itself (שמיני רגל בפני עצמו).

[285] See Dan. 11:31; 2 Macc. 4:52-59.

it to the New Jerusalem, foretold by the Prophets and appearing in the visions of the Apocalypse where the throne of God and of the Lamb is seen to supplant the Temple in the ancient Law.[286]

This triumphalism was manifested in the Jerusalem churches was likewise reflected in other basilicas constructed in other parts of the empire—e.g. Nola—and for the same purpose: to celebrate the Church's triumph and the attendant manifestation of the New Messianic Age. *Clearly both the symbols and the language of Judaism's sacrifical system have been employed and given a Christian expression in both the Nolan and Jerusalem churches!*[287]

Paulinus' Employment of Old Testament and Deutero-Canonical Imagery

Owing to the number of Scriptural paintings adorning the Nolan complex, in Epistula 32 §16 Paulinus was able to say: "If anybody is filled with the holy desire to meditate on the law, he will, while tarrying here, be able to apply himself to the Holy Scriptures." His innovative transference from the literary Sacred Texts to an artistic representation of them likely didn't go unchallenged. He frequently defends his portrayals by saying that they serve the illiterate peasants who frequent the churches (cf., Carmen 27, 545).[288]

---

[286] Robert Milburn, *Early Christian Art & Architecture* (Berkley and Los Angeles: University of California Press, 1988), p. 102

[287] Jacob Neusner says that this violation (so understood from a Jewish viewpoint) of Israel's sanctuary, along with other related events in the 4th century, pressed Israel's sages to write the Talmud. See his *Judaism and Christianity in the Age of Constantine* (Chicago: University of Chicago Press, 1987), pp. 1-28; and his *Scriptures of the Oral Torah* (San Francisco: Harper & Row, 1987), pp. 28-29.

[288] He certainly *wasn't* the first to employ human figures and imperial regalia in Christian representations; nevertheless, owing to his feeling the need to defend his paintings, there's good reason to say that he must have been innovative. It has been suggested that perhaps it was the Oriental themes that were the source of contention among some. Furthermore, given the early Christian dislike for

The Evolution of a Revolution

Paulinus, like other contemporary theologians, was interested in using Old Testament figures to tell the New Testament story. Various courtyards connected the various basilicas at the Nolan complex; and Paulinus likes to decorate them with merging themes from the Old Testament, Inter-Testament (Apocryphal) and New Testament texts. In addition, his interest in connecting the old and the new is also evidenced by his own reflections on the complex's architectural design.

Using the Old Testament to Tell the New Testament's Story

In Carmen 27, 510-530 Paulinus describes the ambulatory at Felix' old church, which he has upgraded from its original humble status. In particular, Paulinus is proud that the murals reflect: (1) all that Moses wrote,[289] and (2) all that Joshua did—Moses prefigures Christ the giver of the New Law and Joshua prefigures Christian conquest, which is an important theme in the era of Paulinus. In Carmen 28, 170-175, Paulinus reflects on the basilica's artwork saying: "the new law has been painted on the old building [(i.e., Felix' new edifice)] and the old law on the new one [(i.e., Apostles' Church)]."[290] This "Law," of course, speaks to Sacred Writ and harks back to Moses—Israel's lawgiver; the Christian interest in this Old Testament Law doesn't extend far beyond usages of it as prooftexts for Jesus' Messiahship. In fact, Christians came to disapprove of the appellation "Hebrew Scripture," opting instead for "Old Testament"—thus accentuating a triumph: the "*New* Testament" over the "*Old* Testament."

Paulinus is fond of the portraiture of Ruth, whom he notes

Greek and Latin (i.e., Pagan) poetry, etc., Paulinus' usage of eloquent Latin may have contributed to the contention: the songs of the poets were said to have been "prepared by demons" (Richard Krautheimer, *Studies in Early Christian Medieval and Renaissance Art* [New York: New York University Press, 1969], pp. 190-191).

[289] Paulinus knows Genesis well. In 610-625 he speaks of Adam, Lot, Isaac, Abimelech, Jacob and Joseph.

[290] Goldschmidt has the order inverted; see Goldschmidt, *Paulinus' Churches at Nola*, p. 71.

The Evolution of a Revolution

separates the periods between the Judges and Israel's united Monarchy in Old Testament times. Ruth's following Naomi, and subsequent departure from Moab, contrasted with Orpah's abandonment of her mother-in-law, serves for Paulinus as a model of the Christian journey—i.e., forsaking all to follow along Christ's narrow way. Paulinus proudly posts Ruth's story; for him she's a sterling example of genuine Christian virtue, and he wants others to reflect on her dedication and the outcome of the noble life she lived.

Merging Old Testament, Inter-Testament and New Testament Texts

Carmen 28 speaks of churches standing fraternally next to each other and yet joined together and adorned with beautiful decorations in marble, painting, paneled ceilings and columns. Depicted are saintly men like Job and Tobias, along with saintly women like Judith and Esther—to name but a few. Job, who was tested by his wounds and Tobias by the loss of his sight, and Judith along with the noble Queen Esther, capture in visual form the story of heroic figures from Israel's past—here reproduced for the Christian "new Israel," the church. Additionally, it's worth noting that the usage of Jewish Deutero-Canonical (i.e., Apocryphal) books is perfectly consistent with the church's appreciation for Jewish inter-testamental folk lore.

Owing to an illiterate general populace, depicting the story of the saints and their virtues by using a visual medium was an acceptable way of telling the Gospel's story.[291]

Paulinus' Reflections on the Architectural Design

Thinking that some may not grasp the spiritual applications from the paintings and/or the Scriptures, Paulinus says:

---

[291] I'm wondering about his justification that the inscriptions served to explain the pictures to the illiterate peasants: how can inscriptions serve those who can't read them?

The Evolution of a Revolution

"If God's lessons from the light of the Word do not open our understanding, let us then at any rate get the examples from the buildings themselves and let the stone and wood be teachers to us dull people" (Carmen 28, 255-265). He then goes on to teach spiritual lessons derived from the buildings in the complex— e.g., using Pauline texts (i.e., Ephesians)[292] and relating them to the joining of old and new basilicas in the complex. Carmen 27, 455-464 also speaks of the joining of the old Felix church to the new Apostles' church. Epistula 32 §15 refers to Paul's joining of the old and the new in Ephesians. This is an important theme for Paulinus, who uses it in the three extant works being considered here.

The Apse Painting in the Apostles' Church
About Apses

In architecture, apses are semicircular or polygonal terminations to the choir, chancel or aisle of a secular or ecclesiastical building. As was the case with basilicas (see above), apses were first used in pre-Christian Roman architecture, where they functioned as enlarged niches holding statues of deities in various temples[293] and shrines.[294] The apse was eventually used in Christian architecture as soon as basilicas began emerging, as a result of the Christian triumph. The assimilation of Greek and Roman styles into Christian houses of worship is quite apparent. Again, this attests to Christianity's new-found prestige: now the church wants to express herself in ways appropriate to the circumstances of the day.

---

[292] Some modern theologians question the Pauline authorship of Ephesians; Paulinus didn't.

[293] *Encyclopaedia Britannica* Vol. I., ed. Philip W. Goetz (Chicago: Encyclopaedia Britannica, Inc., 1987), p. 496.

[294] E.g., at Caesarea Philippi, where a large niche in the rocky side of a mountain housed a statue to Faunus (Pan), the goat-god of shepherds, Jesus told Peter that he'd (or his confession) would be a rock. The point here is that the story took place against the backdrop of a niche housing a deity (Matt. 16:13-18).

The Evolution of a Revolution

Description of the Apse—Epistula 32, §10

A fabulous painting once adorned the vault of the apse of the Apostles' Church at Nola. St. Melania is said to have given Paulinus a genuine piece of Christ's cross—a relic she'd happened upon during her pilgrimage to Jerusalem (Epistula 32 §11). This, along with alleged remains of Biblical personalities—like Andrew, John the Baptist, Thomas and Luke, along with celebrated martyrs like Agricola, Vitalis, Proculus, Euphemia of Chalcedonia and Nazarius (Carmen 27, 400-439)—are said to have resided beneath the altar which stood below the majestic apse painting. Religious relics were important to ancient Christians; a church's prestige was connected, at least in part, to the saints represented therein. Owing to the importance of the basilica's assumed residents—represented by the relics—it's to be expected that Paulinus would spare no expense to honor them.[295] Though lost to us, the apse's imagery may be resurrected by analyzing Paulinus' description of it in Epistula 32 §10, and comparing that imagery to art works from antiquity that have survived.

Epistula 32, §10

Here now is Paulinus' majestic description of the apse:

> [1][296] In full mystery sparkles the Trinity: Christ stands as the Lamb, the voice of the Father thunders from heaven and in the form of a dove the Holy Ghost flows down.
> [2] The Cross is surrounded by a wreath, a bright circle, around which wreath the apostles form again a wreath, the image of whom is expressed in a chorus of doves.
> [3] The holy unity of the Trinity meets in

---

[295] That he had the means to do so argues for his *not* having divested himself of his entire estate.

[296] Brackets indicate numbers that I've placed, which seem to record breaks of thought; the indentations are mine as well.

The Evolution of a Revolution

Christ, Who likewise has the insignia in threefold: being revealed as God by the Fatherly voice and the Ghost, the Cross and the Lamb testifying Him as the sacred sacrificed One, Kingdom and Triumph being indicated by the purple and palm.

[4] He Himself, the Rock of the Church, is standing on a rock from which four seething springs issue, the Evangelists, the living streams of Christ.

Analysis of the Apse
In General

Biblical Motifs: Relationship to Matthew's Gospel

Matthew records[297] the time when Christ appeared for baptism (Matt. 3: 13-17). It was there at the Jordan river when: (1) the heavens were opened and (2) God's Spirit, like a dove, descended upon Him (vs. 16), after which God's voice is said to have thundered: "this is my beloved Son!" (vs. 17). It's this scene at the beginning of Christ's ministry—during the period of His human trek (Php. 2: 7-8)—that Paulinus harks back to, I believe (see below).[298] The pericope in Matthew has often been used as a proof-text for the Triune Godhead, in that all are present: Father, Son and Spirit. This understanding is clearly reflected in the opening verse.

Paulinus has blended scenes from Christ's humble earthly ministry (recorded in Matthew) along with His heavenly exaltation (recorded in Revelation), all of which is done in honor of his confessor Felix and the Apostles, who were said to have resided beneath the apse painting.

Biblical Motifs: Relationship to the Book of Revelation

---

[297] To be politically correct: "according to the text *ascribed* to Matthew."

[298] This interpretation is innovative. Art historians (e.g., Dr. Annemarie Carr) and historical theologians (e.g., Dr. William Babcock) seem to prefer the transfiguration. Why not both the baptism and transfiguration?

The Evolution of a Revolution

In Rev. 17:4, the saints are honored who have come out of the great tribulation and washed their robes in the blood of the Lamb. Likewise, in Rev. 12:11 John speaks of the saints who "overcame the beast by the blood of the Lamb," and "loved not their own lives even unto death." Paulinus' apse painting—adorning the vault covering the remains of the Apostles and his confessor Felix—points to the triumph promised to the martyrs in Revelation. Furthermore, in Rev. 17:7, the Lamb in the midst of the throne is said to "lead the faithful unto fountains of living waters," and in 22:1 John continues this theme, envisioning a "pure river of [the] water of life proceeding out of the throne of God and of the Lamb." Worthy of note is how the apse mosaic likewise depicts the Lamb standing upon a rock, from which flow the waters (see below). Seemingly, there is a connection to these accounts in the book of Revelation.

Though many of the earliest Christians had problems with the Apocalypse,[299] the early Christian emperors apparently did not. Professor F. F. Bruce informs that Constantine attached high importance to the text of Revelation and used its imagery for purposes of his own imperial propaganda.[300] Professor

---

[299] Eusebius, being a bit more critical, listed the Apocalypse under "spurious texts." Of the Revelation of John, he says: "Among the books which are reckoned as spurious should be reckoned... the Apocalypse of John... [noting] some reject it, while others count it among the acknowledged books" (*Ibid.*, pp. 199-200). In evidence of its mixed reviews we note that Revelation is not listed in the canonical list of the Council of Laodicea (c. 363) (*Ibid.*, p. 210) neither is it known by Pseudo-Barnabas (c. 70-130), Clement of Rome (c. 95-97), Ignatus (c. 110), Polycarp (c. 110-150), Diogenetus (c. 150), Cyril of Jerusalem (c. 315-386); or in Marcion (c. 140), Barococcio (c. 206), Apostolic Canons (c. 300), the Tatian Diatessaron (c. 170), or the Old Syriac (c. 200). Nevertheless, it was known at Nicea (c. 325-340), Hippo (393), Carthage (397) and Carthage (419). See Wayne House's *Chronological and Background Charts of the New Testament* (Grand Rapids: Zondervan/Academie Books, 1981), p. 22; from William Nix and Norman Geisler's *Introduction to the Bible* (Chicago: Moody Press, 1986).

[300] Bruce, F.F., *The Canon of Scripture* (Downers Grove, Il.: Intervarsity Press, 1988), p. 205.

The Evolution of a Revolution

Farmer informs that there was a "Martyr's Canon" in which Revelation played a part. For our purposes here, we need only note that it does play a part in imperial art in general, and Paulinus' program of honoring the martyrs, in particular.[301]

Having introduced the Biblical accounts into the conversation, we'll now concern ourselves with a closer examination of the particulars of the apse painting.

The Apse Painting: Verse by Verse
Verse 1
In full mystery sparkles the Trinity: Christ stands as the Lamb, the voice of the Father thunders from heaven and in the form of a dove the Holy Ghost flows down.

Christ as Lamb

Theological usage of lamb imagery reminds one of Old Testament propitiation through the sacrificial system, spoken of earlier in connection with Judaism's Temple and the Nolan basilicas. The LXX uses ἀμνός about one hundred times to mean lambs for *sacrifice*... 1 Enoch 89f., however, uses ἀρήν (the same expression) for the victorious lambs of the Messianic Age. This dual appropriation of the motif (i.e., referencing both suffering and exaltation) is what's likewise reflected in the Apocalypse. Dr. Richard Longnecker opines that both applications of the "Lamb of God" motif—i.e., again, one suffering and then being exalted—seem to have been a unique development in sectors of early Christianity."[302]

---

[301] Farmer, W., and Farkasfalvy, D., *The Formation of the New Testament Canon* (New York: Paulist Press, 1983), pp. 39-41.

[302] Longnecker, R., *The Christology of Early Jewish Christianity* (Grand Rapids: Baker Book House, 1985), p. 51.

The Evolution of a Revolution

Voice of the Father Thundering From Heaven

As has been mentioned already, at Christ's baptism the Lord is quoted as saying: "This is my beloved Son"[303] (Matt 3:17), thus accentuating the unique relationship between the two: God and God's Son. The expression "Son of God" was especially significant to the early Christians (e.g., Matt. 16:16; 26:63; Jn. 11:27; 20:31).[304] It has been observed that the expression was given increased prominence in Matthew—over the other Synoptists[305]—and how it's likewise given extensive treatment in Hebrews much more than in the Pauline corpus. Dr. Longnecker believes that the picture of Christ as "God's beloved Son" was, as he put it, the "initial implication of the primal understanding of the earliest Jewish believers in explication of their conviction of Jesus as the Messiah."[306] In regard to the transmission of that message, that this is God's beloved Son, the following may be helpful.

It was held in Jewish religious circles that the Spirit of God departed following the deaths of Judah's post exilic prophets—Haggai, Zechariah and Malachi. In *Bab. Sanhed.* fol. II.I, Israel's sages state: "The Holy Spirit departed from Israel" (נסתלקה רוח הקדש מישראל), and that "they [(i.e., the Israelites) then] used the *Bath Kol*" (כן משתמשין בבת קול ואעפ).[307] What is meant by the *Bath Kol*? The rabbis explain

---

[303] God also is said to have uttered this at the transfiguration (see n. 38).

[304] Longnecker finds ὁ υἱὸς τοῦ ἀνθρώπου ("Son of Man") cumbersome and inelegant, and says that it was originaly coined in Aramaic as בר אנש or בר נשא. Having suggested this, he then goes on (leaning on Geza Vermes) to posit that "Son of Man" was *not* previously employed, in Jewish literature, as a title with messianic import. (See Longnecker, *The Christology of Early Jewish Christianity*, pp. 85-86) The expression "Son of God" indeed carries just such an import.

[305] E.g., St. Jerome speaks of "the Gospel written in the Hebrew speech which the Nazarenes read" (i.e., Matthew's gospel) as calling Christ the Spirit's "firstborn Son that reignest forever." See his Comm. on Isa. IV (on Isa. 11:2); from Longnecker, *The Christology of Early Jewish Christianity*, p. 53.

[306] Longnecker, *The Christology of Early Jewish Christianity*, pp. 98-99.

[307] The *Jerusalem Talmud*, *Schab.* fol. 8.3, attests to this: "R. Eliezar saith, they

The Evolution of a Revolution

in *Piske Tosaph.* in *Sanhed.* cap. I. 129: "When a voice, or thunder, came out of heaven, another voice came out from it"— i.e., God's voice/ His leading was manifest through various thunderings (כשקול יוצא מתוכו קול אחר). This very image has worked its way atop Paulinus' vault through the account in Matthew.

What's my point in all of this? Simply, Paulinus, is using Jewish apocalyptic/Messianic symbols (as in Matthew) as well as Jewish imagery (as in Revelation) to adorn his church. Fair enough. What Paulinus doesn't known, however, is that Latin Christian citadels are being embellished by symbols on loan from Jewish messianism. *The symbols are being re-employed by churchmen who haven't a clue as to the real origin and meaning of the motifs they are using. Why not? Because they are out of touch with Christianity's Jewish connection.*

Hand of God Extended Downward

Though it doesn't appear in the English translation fo Paulinus' work, Goldschmidt informs that the Latin *genitor coronat,* in 292, 16, speaks of God's hand which was depicted as coming down from the clouds[308] in the apse's painting. The hand then represents God's thundering voice which is depicted in the Matthean account. In his *City of God,* Bk. XII, 24, St. Augustine—Paulinus' contemporary and friend—seems aware of the usage; he says, "God's hand is His power."[309]

The image of God's hand extended doesn't belong to early

---

follow the hearing of the *Bath Kol"* (אחר שמיעת בת קול אר אלעור הולכין). See John Lightfoot's *Commentary on The New Testament From Talmud and Hebraica* (Peabody, Mass.: Hendrickson Publishers, 1989; originally Oxford University Press, 1859), pp. 81-82, where his testimony is accompanied by his typical invectives against the Jews. See also *The Jerome Biblical Commentary,* ed. R. Brown, J. Fitzmeyer, R. Murphy (Englewood Cliffs, NJ: Prentice Hall, 1968), p. 68, for a brief *friendly* confirmation from Catholic scholarship, which has bearing on the baptismal scene in Matt. 3 (see above).

[308] See Goldschmidt, *Paulinus of Nola,* p. 98, 121 for commentary.

[309] Goldschmidt observes that *manus* denotes God's presence and activity in Scripture (cf., e.g. Jn. 10:29; Acts 13:11). See Goldschmidt, *Paulinus of Nola,* p. 121.

The Evolution of a Revolution

Christian imagery (e.g., catacombs), but is said to have developed in late antiquity through Hellenistic import. Here I suggest that possibly the image of God's hand being extended toward His Lamb made it's way into Christian art through Judaism's earlier adaptation of the Hellenistic motif—a contention that I will now seek to support.

The *Akedah* (עקדה, i.e. the "binding")—the pericope in Gen. 22 wherein Abraham takes Isaac to Moriah to offer him up as a sacrifice—has always served as a prototype of Jewish readiness for martyrdom. Interestingly, owing to the fact that there is no reference to Isaac returning with his father in Genesis, it was held in many rabbinic circles that the lad had actually been sacrificed by his father, but was later resurrected from the dead by God.[310]

At Dura Europos, the remains of a third century (A.D.) synagogue have been unearthed alongside that of an early Christian church. Therein, in a Hellenistic Jewish synagogue, we find a picture of God's hand reaching down to restrain Abraham's hand from slaying his only son—through Sarah, that is.[311] As is the case in the Matthean account, the Genesis one only records God's *voice* restraining Abraham, *not* God's hand (see Gen. 22:11). Despite this, *in both cases God's hand is used in place of His voice.* Christian glasswork, dated c. A.D. 400, has been discovered depicting the story of the binding of Isaac. Much like the usage in the synagogue at Dura Europos, these Christian utensils depict God's hand extending downward from the clouds toward Abraham and the ram/lamb about to be sacrificed upon the altar.[312] This gives clear evidence that the figure had worked its way into *Jewish* and *Christian* artistic impressions.[313]

---

[310] See Petuchowski, J., *Heirs to the Pharisees* (New York/London: Basic Books, 1970), pp. 68-75.

[311] *Encyclopaedia Judaica*, Vol. 2. (Jerusalem: Keter Publishing, 1972), p. 485.

[312] Milburn, R., *Early Christian Art and Architecture*, pp. 269-270

[313] See Erwin Goodenough, *Jewish Symbols in the Greco-Roman Period* (Princeton:

The Evolution of a Revolution

There are myriad examples of Christian usages of the story of Isaac's binding (e.g., as an allegory of Jesus Christ's crucifixion).[314] Worthy of note here is the anthropomorphism (i.e., God's hand reaching down) in Jewish and then Christian art, akin to the hand of God which powerfully extends from the clouds in Paulinus' apse mosaic. Once again, Paulinus is employing Jewish understandings—little does he know.

Holy Ghost Coming Down in the Form of a Dove

Dr. Alexander Bruce gives the view of the Church Fathers on the dove's descent at the Jordan baptism. Says he: "The Fathers insisted on the qualities of the dove... philanthropy, patient endurance of wrong, purity, etc."[315] Obviously, this is the stuff that monasticism was made out of, and may account—in part—for Paulinus' interest in the image.

Verse 2

The Cross is surrounded by a wreath, a bright circle, around which wreath the apostles form again a wreath, the image of whom is expressed in a chorus of doves.

Wreath

Foilage from a tree (Nobilis) grown in southern Europe was taken by ancient Greeks and woven into a crown to reward victors in the ancient Pythian games. Mindful of this popular usage, the imagery was immediately employed as an early Christian symbol of triumph (cf., e.g. 1 Cor. 9:25; 1 Thess. 2:19; 2 Tim. 4:8; Jas. 1:12; 1 Pet. 5:4; Rev. 2:10; 3:22; 4:4,10). Used by

---

Princeton University Press, 1988), p. 37, 56.

[314] In literature, cf., e.g. Tertullian, *Adversus Marcionem*, 3:18; Clement of Alexandria, *Paedogogica*, 1:5, see the Junius Bassus sarcophagus and observed the *akedah* scene in connection with calvary, to mention but one of a number of examples.

[315] *The Expositor's Greet Testament*, Vol. I., (Grand Rapids: Eerdmans, 1988), p. 87.

The Evolution of a Revolution

athletes, emperors and then Christians, the laurel wreath was universally understood as a reward for victory.[316]

On the wedding casket of Secundus and Projecta the busts of the husband and wife are enclosed within a wreath[317]; interestingly, pagan themes exist alongside Christian ones on this casket. The Vatican Museum's Sarcophagus 171, which depicts Christ's passion, has the wreath as it's centerpiece.[318] Archbishop Theodore's sarcophagus, in the church of St. Apollinare in Classe, is decorated by a number of wreaths surrounding crosses.[319] The apex of the vault of the presbyterium of S. Vitale, in Ravenna, hosts Christ as the Lamb of God enclosed within a victory wreath.[320] Expensive religious bookcovers had wreathed crosses.[321] We don't lack for examples. Suffice it to say that here Christian triumph was depicted by the laurel wreath (cf., Epistula 32 §14), evidencing the obvious Christian adaptation of the Greco-Roman motif.

Verse 3
The holy unity of the Trinity meets in Christ, Who likewise has the insignia in threefold: being revealed as God by the Fatherly voice and the Ghost, the Cross and the Lamb testifying Him as the sacred sacrificed One, Kingdom and Triumph being indicated by the purple and palm.

Having already spoken on God's voice, the Ghost, the Cross and Lamb, here now we'll simply examine Kingdom and Triumph symblized by purple and palm.

---

[316] *Webster's Seventh New Collegiate Dictionary*, p. 477.

[317] See Robert Milburn's *Early Christian Art and Architecture*, p. 253.

[318] *Ibid.*, p. 69.

[319] *Ibid.*, p. 78.

[320] *The History of Art: Architecture, Painting, Sculpting* ed. Bernard S. Meyers and Trewin Coppelstone (New York: Exeter Books, 1987), p. 227.

[321] E.g., the "Murano Ivory from Constantinople." See Robert Milburn's *Early Christian Art and Architecture*, p. 246.

The Evolution of a Revolution

Purple

While blowing star-dust in Constantine's face at the tricennial orations held in his honor, Eusebius exclaims: "Wherefore let the friend of the All-Ruling God [i.e., Constantine] be proclaimed our sole sovereign... since he alone deserves to wear the royal purple which so becomes him."[322] The wearing of purple, like the wreath, is a well documented royal motif—frequently used in imperial imagery as well as in the Judaism for the Veil in the Holy of Holies.

Palm

In regard to palms and triumph, we note that when Jesus entered Jerusalem, He is said to have been greeted by throngs with branches of palm in hand exclaiming, "Hosanna to the Son of David. Blessed is He who comes in the Name of the Lord!" (Matt. 21:8-9; Jn. 12:13). Let's briefly examine Judaism's usage of the palm in antiquity, and then consider a Christian application.

Originally printed in 1859 on the Oxford University Press, Professor John Lightfoot's *Commentary on the New Testament From the Talmud and Hebraica* represented a Christian attempt to understand a Jewishness of the Gospel. With regard to the לולב (i.e., branch of palm), Dr. Lightfoot observed how the expression "Hosanna to the Son of David" also reads in rabbinic literature as "Branches to the Son of David"; for the binding of branches was sometimes called הושענא (hosanna) by the ancient Jews.[323] Even today, in modern Orthodox Jewish circles, practitioners celebrate the Feast of Tabernacles by encircling the *bimah* (pulpit) while shaking branches of palm

---

[322] H. A. Drake, *In Praise of Constantine: A Historical Study and New Translation of Eusebius' Tricennial Orations* (Berkley/ Los Angeles: University of California Press), p. 89.
[323] Lightfoot, J., *Commentary on the New Testament From Talmud and Hebraica* Vol 2 (Peabody: Hendrickson, 1989), pp. 271-272.

The Evolution of a Revolution

mixed with willow and myrtle and exclaiming, "Hosanna to the Son of David." This is done to commemorate the ancient practice in the Temple[324] and after reciting Ps. 118:25, wherein it says: ברוך הבא בשם יהוה (i.e., "Blessed is He who comes in the name of the Lord"). The point, of course, is that *in the ancient Jewish mind palm and Messianic triumph went hand in hand.*

In his *City of God*, XIII 7, St. Augustine speaks of "the reward of the palm of victory as the just reward for righteouness," evidencing his understanding of the imagery as understood by Christians in his day: the attainment of paradise. The word παράδεισος (*paradeisos*) means "enclosed park" and harks back to the Garden of Eden,[325] when God humanity dwelt in blissful union surrounded by various trees.

There are many examples connecting palm and paradise: the late third century painting in the *arcosolium* of the ceometerium in Rome, shows an orans flanked by trees, depicting paradise[326]; in the interior of Sta. Constanza in Rome, the apse mosaic in the north ambulatory depicts Christ on a rock from which four streams are flowing,[327] and there too we note the palms in paradise; trees decorate the mosaic apse at St. Apollinare in Classe, as well as the Mausoleum of Galla Placidia's mosaic of the Good Shepherd in Ravenna[328]; palms also were used in Roman catacombs.[329] These are but a few of the many examples; they'll, I assume, no doubt suffice to prove the point.

In sum, it may be observed that palms were used to depict the triumph of David's Son, the Messiah, and the return to

---

[324] See Eliyahu Kitov, *The Book of Our Heritage* Vol. 1. (Brooklyn: Feldheim Publications, 1978), pp. 201-208.

[325] *Webster's Seventh New Collegiate Dictionary*, p. 610. The word was first used by Xenophon to denote the parks of Persian kings and nobles. (*Vine's Expository Dictionary of New Testament Words*, p. 840.)

[326] *The History of Art: Architecture, Painting, Sculpting,*p. 196.

[327] *Ibid.*,p. 201.

[328] See Robert Milburn's *Early Christian Art and Architecture,* p. 174 and p. 177.

[329] *Ibid.*, p. 37.

The Evolution of a Revolution

paradise—the Garden of Eden. It's a place that Christ Himself reentered, and a place that the Church—through its ambassadors—now invites others to enter.

Verse 4

He Himself, the Rock of the Church, is standing on a rock from which four seething springs issue, the Evangelists, the living streams of Christ.

Stone

Jewish literature abounds with references to foundation stones (אבן שתיה).[330] The image of a Lamb upon a stone is indeed interesting, and has a history in the Jewish sacrificial cult—as well as others. The Jerusalem Temple's altar was a tiered object. The uppermost part of the altar was called הראל (*har'el*), meaning the "Mount of God"[331]; and it was there, in Jerusalem, that the sacrifical lambs were consumed. Certainly, a sacrificial lamb on a rock echos this image and harks back to the sacrificial cult and propiation. Though the image of Christ as a lamb was eventually condemned in the East,[332] it apparently remained popular in the West.

In the Crypt of the Saints' catacomb of St. Peter and St. Marcellinus in Rome, the Divine Lamb is depicted as standing on a knoll, from which four heavenly rivers flow,[333] much as it was in the Nolan picture. As has been noted, in the interior of Sta. Constanza in Rome, the apse mosaic in the north ambulatory depicts Christ on a rock from which four streams are flowing. Four streams flow from paradise in Genesis.

---

[330] Cf., *Manual of Discipline* 8.4; Baby. Yoma 54a; 1QH 6.25-27; 7.8-9; 1QS 5.6; 9.5f.; j. Sanh. 29a; Exod. R. 15.7; Lev. R. 20. 4., in *The Christology of Early Jewish Christianity*, p. 52.

[331] Some have opted for a relationship between this and the Babylonian "Temple Towers" called Ziggurat. W. F. Albright conjectured that there might be a connection with the Akkadian *crallu*, a poetic name for the netherworld.

[332] See Cyril Mango, *The Art of the Byzantine Empire* (Toronto: University of Toronto Press, 1986), p. 123, 139.

[333] *The History of Art: Architecture, Painting, Sculpting,* p. 198.

The Evolution of a Revolution

Mindful of this, we note the following: here, in paradise restored—i.e., in the Christian church—the four rivers again flow.[334]

Summary

In Christian basilicas, Jewish literature, faith and practice were reinterpreted for non-Jewish Christians. Latin Christian art, architecture and literature employed OT and NT themes and personalities and welded them together with imperial Greco-Roman motifs. Together they told the story of the triumph of the Gentile Christian church.

---

[334] The application to the four rivers being the Gospels' speaks to a past controversy over the validity of all four Gospels. Marcion, a Gnostic, insisted that only a redacted version of Luke represented authentic Christian teaching—a notion that was eventually voted down.

Conclusion

At the outset, in my introduction, I informed that I would leave it up to my readers to determine whether or not there were any pearls in this book. As you may have noticed, in the introduction, I held out no guarantee that you would be blessed through the acquisition and digestion of this book—though I said that I hoped that you would be; and I made no claim that God inspired me to write the book—though I hoped you would find His hand in it in some way. Having read *The Evolution of a Revolution: Reflections on Ancient Christianity in its Judaistic, Hellenistic and Romanistic Expressions,* and thus having joined with me in journeying back to the ancient world, you are now, I believe, in a position to make some sort of determination about the book's value.

As far as I am concerned, I am cognizant of a number of weaknesses in my account of ancient Christianity. In covering the early church, for example, I could have discussed the *Dead Sea Scrolls* and noted the similarities in the nomenclature employed therein with the NT's vocabulary. I virtually ignored this fertile field here. Additionally, I am aware of the fact that my coverage of Hellenic influences on Palestinian and non-Palestinian Christianity was quite scanty. Furthermore, in this regard, I seriously wonder whether my readers would have been better served had I covered some of the major events between the first century and fourth century. In sum, as I reflect on my book, I am reminded of the fact that there is much that I didn't say—*perhaps too much.*

Of course, on the other hand, I never promised to give a comprehensive treatment of early Christian history—others, more capable than I, have done that quite well already. In this volume, I only really wanted my readers to appreciate the following: *Originally, in the early first century, Christianity—so called—was a Jewish movement; by the fourth century, however, Jewish expressions were eschewed altogether by a Roman church bent on proving that it had replaced Israel in God's economy.* There you have it—the entire book in one simple sentence.

If you opt to agree with me that the above statement is correct—and, for that matter, you may feel free to not agree with me—you may feel pressed to ask: *What are the implications?* This is another question—and an excellent one, I might add; however, it is a question that you will have to answer for yourself. *Think about it!*

—The End